Endorsements

If you want to know how we can most effectively win the world for Christ read Mark
can change your church and your life! Once you begin to take the steps encouraged
God glorify himself through expanding His Kingdom in the United States and around the world!

Rev. Paul Becker,
Founder and President, Dynamic Church Planting International

Mark Williams has captured his passionate ministry of developing a church planting movement in his book, *Winning The World For Christ: The Untapped Potential of Daughter Church Planting*. Mark has taught this his STTARR Process in the U.S., Africa, India and elsewhere and has seen it work. The book is full of testimonies from all these localities to the power involved in this simple approach to church planting. Mark believes in this method. I believe in Mark. I recommend this book to leaders-especially those who want to start a dynamic church planting movement in their regions and countries. Mark and his team at Dynamic Church Planting International are willing to come and help you start just such a church planting movement. Get this very practical book. Get involved in the best evangelistic method available-church planting.

Dr. J. Robert Clinton
Professor of Leadership
School of InterCultural Studies
Fuller Theological Seminary
Pasadena, California, USA

Dr. Mark Williams has done every church planter a huge favor by writing *Winning the World for Christ: The Untapped Potential of Daughter Church Planting*. With the mind of a fine scholar, the excellence of an outstanding teacher, and the remarkable example of a great church planter himself, Mark has written a book that will encourage and equip church planters all over the world.

Rev. David Godoy
DCPI Latin America World Zone Leader
Uberlandia, Brazil

I've been involved in church planting and the training of church planters for over two decades in West Africa, and this book stands out as a uniquely valuable resource. It is full of Scriptural authority and practical application.

I'm not surprised that Mark has written such a fine book, since I have co-labored with him in various ministries over the years. He is a man with a huge heart for the harvest of souls! I recommend unreservedly this book to everyone: read it, meditate on it, and practice it, to the glory of God!

Rev. Christophe Dewanou
Director of Missions Foursquare Gospel Church Republic of Benin
Coordinator of West and Central Africa Dawn Ministries
Benin, West Africa

This book combines a zeal for planting daughter churches with a conciliatory acknowledgment of the birth pains involved. There was a day when I was pushing Mark to plant a daughter church. Now he's written a book about it.

Dr. Bob Logan
CoachNet International Ministries
Alt Loma, California, USA

In *Winning the World for Christ: The Untapped Potential of Daughter Church Planting*, Mark Williams makes the case and provides the tools for the most effective church planting possible. Church multiplication is a mandate in Scripture. This book is a powerful service to all pastors and even long established churches in living out that mandate.

Dr. Ross Chenot
Church Resource Minister
Transformation Ministries
California, USA

Mark Williams has planted two churches, daughtered five churches, including the church I pastor. He has also coached the mother/daughter process for hundreds of churches around the world. His insight, experience, and straight-forward communication style make this essential reading for anyone planting or daughtering a church.

Dr. Hal Seed
Founding Pastor,
New Song Community Church
Oceanside, California, USA

There are few things more important or closer to Christ's heart than advancing the kingdom of God through the planting of new churches. That is why I am excited about Mark William's practical and focused contribution to modern church planting in *Winning the World for Christ*. This book was not written from the ivory tower of conjecture and speculation, but has been birthed through the insight and acumen of an experienced church planter. Dr. Williams knows the challenges and the joys of seeing God replicate the "Acts template" in the 21st century. I trust that God will use *Winning the World for Christ* to motivate this generation of Christians to do the same.

Dr. Mike Fabarez
Author of *Preaching that Changes Lives* (Thomas Nelson, 2002)
Senior Pastor of Compass Bible Church
Aliso Viejo, California, USA

Mark Williams' straight forward presentation of this material is theologically sound, methodologically doable, and truly practical. As the church becomes a smaller and smaller percentage of the overall population, following Mark's prescription will help reverse this disturbing trend. Mother - daughter church planting is proving to be one of the most successful models for future church plant strategies. Mark's design and plan for this structure deserves a hard look from all of us in the ministry of evangelizing through church planting.

Rev. Phil Spry
Church Plant Strategies
Clayton, North Carolina, USA

In the 80's, my wife Yadira and I decided to plant a church in one of the middle class neighborhoods of Bogota, Colombia. We had no formal church planting training—only a great desire to reach the lost. We labored, struggled, and with much prayer survived and planted a church that soon gave birth to seven daughter churches.

In the 1990's we came to live in Colorado Springs to serve as missionaries under Dawn Ministries. I discovered that 10% of the city was Hispanic, but only 2% of the Hispanic population was attending any kind of church. With the Lord's prompting, my wife and I decided to establish a church, again with only the skills we had and our deep desire to reach people for Christ.

I wish I had Mark Williams' book with me in those years of church planting! It could have saved me many headaches and sleepless nights. With the tools the book provides, I would have been a better role model for my disciples. Mark Williams' book is right on target. **It is meant for such a time as this!** The principles in this book will help you join God in this exciting time of harvest!

To Him be all the Glory!

Rev. Berna Salcedo
Dawn Ministries

Winning the World for Christ:
The Untapped Potential of Daughter Church Planting

By Mark Alan Williams

Dynamic Church Planting International (DCPI) is a training mission dedicated to reaching the world for Christ by multiplying church planting around the world. DCPI is driven by its vision: *"Equipping leaders to plant one million dynamic churches to reach the world for Christ."*

Dynamic Church Planting Resources is the publishing ministry of DCPI.

Published by Dynamic Church Planting Resources
PO Box 4119
Oceanside, CA 92052-4119
USA

In association with
Brilliant Printers Pvt. Ltd. – India
#18 & 19, L G Halli, R M V II Stage
Bangalore – 560 094, INDIA

ISBN: 978-1-935221-00-5

Unless otherwise indicated, all Scripture quotations are from the HOLY BIBLE, NEW INTERNATIONAL VERSION®. NIV®. Copyright© 1973, 1978, 1984 by International Bible Society. Used by permission of Zondervan Publishing House. All rights reserved.

Design and layout by Melanie Myers Design
design@melaniemyers.net

Printed in Bangalore, India

Please contact us at
DCPI
www.dcpi.org
service@dcpi.org

Dedication

This book is dedicated to "my three sons" Gabe, Danny and Ben.
I love you and I am proud of you. You are a wonderful joy to Carolyn and me.

Acknowledgments

This book is really the result of the work and contributions of hundreds of supporters, ministry workers and encouragers. Thank you to all who have so significantly impacted my life and the Kingdom.

Special thanks first to my wonderful wife Carolyn who after almost 30 years of marriage is an incredible blessing to me.

Thanks to the thousands of staff of DCPI around the world for all you are doing to advance the vision of a million.

Special thanks to Don and Grace Modglin for their support of this project.

Thanks to Dionne Carpenter for her editing expertise and Jim Carpenter for assisting in putting this book into publication.

My Mentors

Every life is impacted immensely by those who mentor them. My most memorable mentors have been:

My parents, Claude and Barbara Williams, set an incredible example for me. Perhaps the finest Christians I have known…and I saw them up close and personal.

The Snook girls: Ellen, Sandy & Bonnie, one of whom led me to Jesus in a little Sunday School class in Reynoldsburg, Ohio.

Norris "Mosey" Miller who mentored me in guitar and Junior High Sunday School.

Bobby Clinton, Bob Wagonblot and Tim Newkirk who led Senior High youth group and Bible classes.

Don Sweeting, example and lifelong friend.

David Nawroki and Gerry Edmonds, concert band leaders and models in unique ways.

Dr. George Sweeting, more than just the president of Moody Bible Institute, a mentor and hero.

Josh McDowell, mentor and champion.

Jim Carpenter, earliest church planting mentor and lifelong friend.

Dave Proffitt and Mel Holland, early church planting mentors.

Phil and Virginia Feliciano who were so central to our church plant that it actually began in their home.

Bob Logan, whose mentoring was truly remarkable and timely.

Floyd "Mac" McElveen, the greatest "soul-winner" I know.

Paul Becker has been and is a fantastic mentor and friend.

Eric Helmbold and Cathy Becker, coworkers and real friends.

Hal Seed and Scott Evans, great friends with great insight.

Dan and Debby Proctor, my computer mentors.

Dr. Jayakumar, from whom I have learned so much about international ministry.

Charlie Bradshaw, Paul Eshleman and Frank DeMattia, recent mentors who are taking me and our ministry to higher levels.

Table of Contents

Foreword

By Dr. Ed Stetzer

In 2004, I did a study for the North American Mission Board on the state of church planting in North America. The report of this study can be found on my website, www.newchurches.com. From this study, I discovered what everyone supposed at the time… church planting was on the rise in North America.

From a survey of 124 organizations, a staggering 122 organizations reported an increase in interest in church planting. We did an update of that study in 2007 and found the pace increasing—Warren Bird and I did research (reported in Rev! Magazine) that shows there were more churches planted in 2007 than closed. With the great increase in conferences and materials on church planting, it could be correctly surmised that interest in church planting in North America continues to grow. I believe the Kingdom is better for this growth. But however you see it, church planting has become the "next big thing."

That's why Dr. Mark Williams' book *Winning The World For Christ: The Untapped Potential of Daughter Church Planting* is such a timely addition to the church planting movement. Instead of believing that one church should be the only representation of the Kingdom in a community, Mark Williams has sought to increase his (and your) impact through mother-daughter church planting. Himself a two-time church planter, Mark has led churches to multiply by planting daughter churches. Some of these daughter churches went on to plant churches of their own. Currently serving as a trainer of church planters and as a cheerleader for church planting through his position with Dynamic Church Planting International, Mark Williams has proven himself as a champion of the effort to lead churches to plant more churches.

Williams is a firm believer in the need to plant churches. By his own example of leading his church plants to reproduce by planting daughter churches, Williams has proven that he believes the most effective way to increase the spread of the Gospel is for churches to give birth to churches.

The Role of Evangelism in Church Planting

Around the world there is a growing awareness that new churches are more effective at evangelism than existing churches.

Though it can be tempting to plant churches populated by people stolen from other congregations, true biblical church planting is evangelistic. This was the case with the early church in the book of Acts. The New Testament Church was birthed through the preaching of Christ to the very people who had cheered on Christ's crucifixion. With this preaching of the Gospel, we see where thousands came to faith in Christ. These thousands were grafted into Christ and became the beginning of a great movement to reach the world for the Savior.

Somewhere along the line, we've gotten off track and lost focus on our very purpose of reaching the lost. We like to point the fingers and say this is the fault of existing churches, but the reality is this is all too true in many church plants as well. We've forgotten the urgency of the Gospel. I'm not so sure that we can even say a new church plant is being true to the biblical model if it isn't intentionally praying and working towards making Christ known to those who don't yet have the hope of Christ living in them.

Obviously for those seeking to reach into the unchurched world, there are many ways of starting churches. Some planters strike out on their own while others are sent out by mission sending agencies, denominations, or associations. In *Win the World for Christ, the Untapped Potential for Daughter Church Planting*, Williams leads us to see that planting daughter churches is one of the most effective and cost-effective ways churches can evangelize our unbelieving communities and beyond.

The Need Is Great and the Time Is Now

It's a common fallacy in the United States that we don't need new churches. But demographic research proves otherwise. In many parts of the US, 50 – 97% of the community attend church only occasionally, and most are unchurched altogether. Armed with an understanding of the lostness of North America, Williams stresses the need for starting churches that will engage the unsaved with the Gospel. With successful examples of church planting churches all across North America and the world, Williams shows that our situation isn't hopeless. With mother-daughter church planting, the potential for church multiplication and evangelism is endless.

Reversing a Church's Inward Focus

Like any organization, churches have a natural tendency to look inward. We may do a somewhat decent job of forwarding some mission dollars to causes in another state or country, but we tend to forget that there is a growing and significant population of lost and unchurched people all around us. If left unchecked and uncorrected, our inward focus will cause the church to lose its evangelistic fervor, resulting in the loss of people and financial resources, eventually leading the church to close its doors.

We are experiencing an accelerated decline of evangelistic zeal in churches throughout North America. Without a change of direction, these churches will be added to the growing rolls of shuttered churches when their faithful few pass away. Without visionary leading, church plants will also lose their evangelistic potential and they too, will one day have to lock their doors for good.

Some pastors would say this isn't their problem. They are leading their churches to give to missions, grow by transfer growth, build new buildings, add staff, and they are seeing the baptisms and salvations of church members' children and grandchildren…what more could they ask for? Such churches can be lured to a slow, tranquilizing eternal sleep.

I agree wholeheartedly with Williams that one of the greatest ways to keep a church focused on the Gospel is to lead a church to plant churches. Planting churches can be expensive, but it doesn't have to be. Planting churches can be done by large churches, but small churches can plant as well. Planting churches can be (and should be) done to reach unreached people groups all across the world, including the growing unchurched population of North America, Europe and other "Christian" areas. Just as new members can breathe new life into a church, the multiplication process of giving birth to daughter churches can breathe new life into a congregation.

But My Questions, What about My Questions?

When should churches start churches? How big does a church have to be before it can plant another church? What kind of financial and people resources should a church commit to starting a daughter church? Can a church send some of its problem people to start a new church? Is one church plant enough? Should churches only start daughter churches oversees, or should churches consider planting churches around the street corner? How can small churches start churches? Where do we find leadership for the churches that need to be planted? Can't we just start a video venue? …These and other questions are all addressed in this book.

Williams' STTARR PROCESS, explained in Part Two, will be very helpful to your efforts of starting daughter churches through your church.

Obviously when an existing church, old or new, considers any endeavor as detailed as planting a church, much care and attention must be given not only to the details, but also to bringing church members on board. I believe Williams' approach to rallying the church around the vision for a new church plant is one of the best approaches out there.

Prayer Points and Action Steps

As you read this book, take advantage of the Prayer Points and Action Steps at the end of each chapter. Don't cheat yourself and don't cheat potential growth for the Kingdom by rushing past these elements. Pastors and church planters can have a nasty habit of getting so excited about something that we forget to adequately pray and to consider every angle of a growth proposition.

Conclusion

Church planting is a powerful and important endeavor. I believe it is ordained of God. Yet, I also know from experience that it is amazingly difficult. But, you can do it. Just be sure to pray. Take the time to gather a team around you who will pray with you. You will even see benefits from working through these Prayer Points and Action Steps with them. Not only will you be better for this, your church planting process will as well.

Open Your Heart and God Will Lead

You are on the right track. Even if you are still a little skeptical about leading your church to plant churches, I trust that you will be open to whatever God may say to you as you read this book, study the Word, and stay on your knees. May God greatly bless you as you seek His leading and search for the possibilities He may bring your way in leading your church to be more missional as a church planting church.

Thank you, Mark, for leading by example as you planted churches that became mother and grandmother churches. Thank you for giving us this great resource. Thanks for the challenge to dream big and to do big things for God. I pray many will follow God's leading and make Christ more famous as they are challenged by the words you've written here.

Ed Stetzer, Ph.D.
www.newchurches.com

PART ONE

WHY YOUR CHURCH
CAN AND SHOULD
BIRTH DAUGHTER CHURCHES

Chapter 1

Family Pictures: Then and Now

KARRY AND SABRINA

I looked across the restaurant table into the eyes of a conflicted man. Karry had been raised an atheist, but now was considering a new direction—becoming a follower of Jesus Christ.

I met Karry through his wife Sabrina. When we planted a church in their area we wanted to get community feedback on what to call our church. So I did a survey outside grocery stores asking people to pick their favorite name. Sabrina took the survey and gave me her address to receive information when we started services. Sabrina and her three young girls began attending our church regularly. Soon she recommitted her life to Christ and became a member.

Sabrina talked Karry into coming to church on Christmas and Mother's Day. He began to rethink whether God existed and if he needed to know Him through Jesus Christ. So in the restaurant that day he peppered me with questions about the proof for the existence of God, the veracity of the Bible and the need for salvation.

A few months later I sat in the back of the church when my retired missionary friend, Jim Halbert, gave the message. He spoke about Abraham's willingness to sacrifice his son Isaac on an altar and how God gave His Son to die for our sins. Watching the crowd I wondered how Karry might respond. I soon found out when Jim closed the service in prayer. Tears rolled down Karry's cheeks as he walked to the back of that middle school auditorium. He surrendered his life to Jesus that day! Karry turned from hell to heaven. Today, some eight years later, Karry walks with Jesus, leads Bible studies and teaches children's Sunday School.

During the first two and a half years at our new church, 115 people like Karry professed faith in Christ. Others like Sabrina rededicated their lives to Christ. While most long established churches rarely see this kind of response, in new churches this level of spiritual harvest is common.

HOLLY

Thirteen people professed faith in Christ on our opening Sunday. One of them was a single mother named Holly. She had been in such deep despair she contemplated suicide. Holly even thought that if she took her own life, she might take her three children's lives as well.

But one day she got a card in the mail announcing the start of our church. The name caught her eye: New Hope Community Church. "New hope. That's what I need," Holly thought. That first Sunday when I preached to the crowd of 220 people I offered the hope of Christ. Holly, along with her three children, gave her life to Jesus that day. Later she testified, "It was just the most wonderful feeling. Nothing has been the same since." Since then Holly has grown dramatically in her walk with Christ. Soon after her conversion Holly began to volunteer in the church office where she serves to this day.

GHANA

As I write these words I sit in a hotel room in Kumasi, Ghana in West Africa. Our team has just finshed two weeks of training Ghanians leaders how to start new churches more effectively. Their zeal is magnificent. With little training and scant resources but tons of commitment and love for Christ, these Africans get the job done. Pastors often start four or more branch or daughter churches within just a few years. Several testify that through our time with them they now dream bigger visions for church planting evangelism. They now hope to train leaders to plant at least a hundred churches in their lifetimes.

I shiver with excitement when I think of that happening. Already Ghana is more Christian than my own homeland (the USA) in many ways. While their air, water and landscape are sometimes polluted, their environment is cleaner and more wholesome than in the US. Evidences of Christian faith flourish. Perhaps half the businesses have names like the following: "By His Grace Snack Shack," "Clap for Jesus Fashion Glass and Aluminum Fixtures," "God of Grace and Beauty Dress Shop," "Jesus Cares Supermarket," "In Him is Life Electronics," and "Look to Jesus Import and Export." We were blessed just reading the business names and billboards!

When I look at my own homeland—the USA, and many other "post-Christian" nations, I see great spiritual stagnation and moral decline. It is hard to write these words, but it is the truth. We will continue to decline unless we take steps to stop it. We need God to work another first century miracle of community-transforming evangelism in our day. But what is our part? What does the Lord want us to do? The tale of two cities gives us the answer.

JERUSALEM: AN UNINTENTIONAL MOTHER CHURCH

Our Lord Jesus gave us the Mission Statement for the church in Acts 1:8. "But you will receive power when the Holy Spirit comes on you; and you will be my witnesses in Jerusalem, and in all Judea and Samaria, and to the ends of the earth." Notice that He told the disciples to spread the Good News in four ever-widening concentric localities: first in Jerusalem, then Judea, then Samaria and finally to the ends of the earth.

The theme of this Mission Statement applies today—we have a responsibility to share Christ to these same four localities.

Our Jerusalem = our hometown

Our Judea = our local region

Our Samaria = our cross-cultural neighbors

To the ends of the earth = people from completely different cultures than ours

Jesus gave this clear command early in the life of the church, birthed in Jerusalem. But it took a

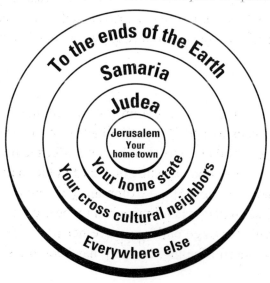

long time for the disciples to reach beyond Jerusalem to fulfill the Great Commission. You can flip through the accounts of Acts 2, 3, 4, 5, 6 and 7 without seeing any movement beyond Jerusalem. All the while the church in Jerusalem enjoyed signs and wonders, fantastic growth and fabulous fellowship.

> Every day they continued to meet together in the temple courts. They broke bread in their homes and ate together with glad and sincere hearts, praising God and enjoying the favor of all the people. And the Lord added to their number daily those who were being saved. (Acts 2:46-47)

Not only did the church grow by 3,000 on the day of Pentecost, it continued to grow in remarkable ways. "But many who heard the message believed, and the number of men grew to about five thousand" (Acts 4:4). Later the record says, "So the word of God spread. The number of disciples in Jerusalem increased rapidly, and a large number of priests became obedient to the faith" (Acts 6:7).

By now about eight years had passed without any significant outreach beyond their hometown of Jerusalem.[1] I find that surprising, but not unusual. In fact, to my own shame I confess that it took about that long before my first church plant began to move out from our comfortable "Jerusalem" to fulfill the Great Commission.

Everything changed for the early church when opposition arose against the godly ministry of Stephen. Soon he became the first martyr of the church. While this was a tragedy, something magnificent came from it. Acts 8:1 (easy to remember since it is the reverse of Acts 1:8) tells us, "And Saul was there, giving approval to his death. On that day a great persecution broke out against the church at Jerusalem, and all except the apostles were scattered throughout Judea and Samaria" (Acts 8:1). Notice two things about this verse:

1. Everyone but the apostles scattered from Jerusalem. Where did they go? To Judea and Samaria! Due to persecution, they began to fulfill the Great Commission.

2. A man named Saul assisted in Stephen's martyrdom. Later this persecutor of the church became one of its greatest champions after his conversion to Christ. We know him better by his new name, Paul.

What happened in Jerusalem illustrates *Unintentional* **Daughter Church Planting.** This happens when one church gives birth to another church "by accident."

Unintentional daughter church planting can happen in several different ways:

1. Persecution. While not a problem in many countries, believers around the world have been scattered by persecution often resulting in evangelism and daughter church planting.

2. Church Splits. When I was a senior in high school, the church my family attended suffered a heart-breaking split. But out of that tragedy came a second church. Sometimes church splits even produce megachurches, such as the Emmanuel Faith Community Church in Escondido, California, which today averages about 5,000 in attendance.

3. The Call of God on a Church Staff Member. God may lay a church planting vision on the heart of a church staff member. My friend Dennis Larkin was a Youth Pastor when God called him to plant a church. Even though his church hadn't planned to daughter a church, the people embraced the idea and became an unintentional mother church.

4. Adoption. Sometimes a fledgling church looks around for a mother and approaches an established congregation asking for help: "Will you be my mother?"

5. A Surprise Pregnancy. While my wife Carolyn and I tried to plan when she would become pregnant, we discovered that we did not have as much control as we thought. Likewise, sometimes God lays the dream of a new church on the hearts of the members of a church body, not the leadership. Perhaps these lay people want to start a church in an area closer to their homes. Whatever the motivations, as a "surprise pregnancy" develops, church leaders can embrace it, ignore it or sometimes even attempt a church "abortion." That's right; they actually try to kill the baby church before it is born. I believe that these baby church pregnancies should be accepted and nurtured to their full potential.

6. The Legacy of a Dying Church. Sometimes a church in the process of disbanding will designate that their remaining assets be used to plant churches. New life comes from death. One Southern California church closed its doors after a long and gallant history. But thirteen new churches started using the proceeds from the sale of its property.

ANTIOCH: AN INTENTIONAL MOTHER CHURCH

When the believers disbursed because of the persecution in Jerusalem, some of them planted a church in Antioch of Syria:

> Now those who had been scattered by the persecution in connection with Stephen traveled as far as Phoenicia, Cyprus and Antioch, telling the message only to Jews. Some of them, however, men from Cyprus and Cyrene, went to Antioch and began to speak to Greeks also, telling them the good news about the Lord Jesus. The Lord's hand was with them, and a great number of people believed and turned to the Lord (Acts 11:19-21).

That church in Antioch became perhaps the most significant church in history. Why? Because we read in Acts 13:1-3:

> In the church at Antioch there were prophets and teachers: Barnabas, Simeon called Niger, Lucius of Cyrene, Manaen (who had been brought up with Herod the tetrarch) and Saul. While they were worshiping the Lord and fasting, the Holy Spirit said, 'Set apart for me Barnabas and Saul for the work to which I have called them.' So after they had fasted and prayed, they placed their hands on them and sent them off.

I see four significant points in this passage:

1. This Antioch is the same Antioch mentioned above, a church begun unintentionally because of the persecution of believers in Jerusalem.

2. Saul is the same Saul who helped to persecute the church, which prompted the planting of a church in Antioch.

3. This marked the first time a church <u>intentionally</u> sent leaders to plant new churches in order to evangelize the lost.

4. This daughtering endeavor was birthed by the call of God during a time of worshipping and fasting, then quickly carried out after more prayer and fasting.

In one sense, every church in existence today traces its history back to Antioch. Churches in Europe and the Americas owe a debt to that great pioneering church. Its missionaries, Barnabas and Saul sailed west. The Gospel spread westward toward the westernmost part of Asia. Then via the Macedonian call to "come over and help us" the Gospel spread into Europe, and later to the "New World."

Other believers like the Apostle Thomas traveled eastward and planted churches throughout Asia and India and others traveled south into Africa. While some of these churches may have started because of persecution or other unintentional circumstance, most church planters branched out because of their obedience to the Great Commission and to the call of the Holy Spirit.

The Antioch church illustrates *Intentional* **Daughter Church Planting** —churches planting daughter congregations as a deliberate effort instead of by accident.

This deliberate daughter church planting can use different models:

1. The Missionary Model. This happened in Acts 13 and since then has happened in thousands of churches as missionaries have been sent out to spread the Good News.

2. The "Send a Team Nearby" Model. Apparently the church in Ephesus used this model to plant the other six churches mentioned in Revelation 2 and 3. On a study trip to Ephesus I learned that in Roman times a circular Roman road connected those seven cities. The husband and wife team of Aquila and Priscilla probably started the church in Ephesus (see Acts 18).[2] After its founding, Christians went out in teams to start new churches in the other six cities.

Likewise, most churches can find at least a few hardy members who, if challenged and called by God, would willingly leave the comfort of their own fellowship to help plant a church in a nearby area.

3. The "Raise up a Timothy" Model. Barnabas mentored Paul who became probably the greatest church planter ever. He became a great mentor to many other church planters; men like Timothy, Silas, Luke, and Epaphras.

One of the best modern mentors of church planters that I know of is Ralph Moore. His Hope Chapel Movement has grown to over 200 churches on six continents. Most of these churches got their start from lay people who had been trained in church planting methodology through his church.

4. The "Let My People Go" Model. Like the "Send a Team Nearby" model, this approach sends people, except in this case the church may send 20% or more of its congregation to plant a daughter church. For example, in 1998 Eastside Wesleyan Church in Albuquerque, New Mexico got the vision to daughter a new church on the west side of town. From a congregation that averaged 71 people on a good Sunday, they sent 24 people and $5,000 to start the new church.[3] Their vision produced eternal results. Now two churches thrive, reaching more than either could do alone.

5. The "Let My Pastor Go" Model. Sometimes a church sends their pastor to start a new church. In 1994 I had the privilege of planting a new church within a 15-minute drive from my first church plant. Sometimes churches invest more than just the pastor. In 1985 the First Church of God in Tulsa, OK averaged 55 people in attendance. They sent their pastor and 25 people, plus a few thousand dollars to plant a new church nearby. This was NOT A SPLIT—but rather intentional daughter church planting.[4]

6. The "Partner Church" Model. In this paradigm, one or more churches work together with another church to plant a daughter church. Thus they become partners, but not the mother church. Assistance may come in many forms: short-term workers, a temporary meeting place, office space, funding, oversight, and so on. One of my churches assisted a Spanish-speaking congregation by allowing them to use our church building on Sunday afternoons.

My own involvement in daughter church planting came at the urging of my friend and mentor, Bob Logan. He mentored me through my first church plant. One day he caught me off guard when he challenged me, "Mark, now that your church is up and going, it is time to start planting daughter churches." While I did not respond much outwardly, inwardly I reacted strongly, "Forget it Bob." I interpreted his challenge as a suggestion that I sacrifice my own ministry to make another ministry successful.

I had been stung by the Killer B's, of church success: Bodies, Bucks (dollars) and Buildings. I evaluated the success of my own ministry by measuring how many of these B's I gathered in my church. I failed to realize that by the standards of the Great Commission, (remember those concentric circles?) I hadn't yet pushed beyond my Jerusalem to pursue the other mission fields.

I did tell Bob that I would pray about it and when I did, the Lord gripped my heart. I realized that I was actually being selfish with the resources that God had given our church. I opened my heart to the idea that our church might produce children. Before long, Paul Becker, our denominational church planting leader, brought a church planter to my home. I told him that if the Lord led him to our area, I would help out by sending people to assist him.

Not long afterward, Hal Seed moved to our area and I helped him gather people from our church to start the new work. Eventually we sent about 15% of our congregation to help his church plant. That church has since led hundreds of people to Christ and grown to about four times bigger than the attendance at the "mother" church. I am thrilled with what God has done to reach our Judea!

That mother church went on to give birth to other daughter churches and partner with more. The combined impact of all these churches far exceeds the impact that our church would have had if we had not helped to start other churches.

CHAPTER SUMMARY

The New Testament church in Jerusalem began to fulfill Christ's Great Commission when they moved beyond their comfort zone to plant new churches. Sometimes they did this on purpose, sometimes accidentally. We too should move beyond our comfort zone to find the people like Holly and Karry who need to hear the Good News. In the next chapter we will discover the most natural and effective way to reach our world for Christ.

Prayer Points: How you can pray about what you learned in this chapter.

- Pray for wisdom to reach your Jerusalem, Judea, Samaria and the ends of the earth to help fulfill the Great Commission.

- Pray for intentional church planting rather than planting through church splits, persecution or other difficult means.

- Pray that the 3 Killer B's (bodies, bucks and buildings) won't hinder you or your church leaders.

Action Steps: What you can do to implement the steps in this chapter.

- Review the points in this chapter.

- Think about the churches you have attended. Did they start by accident or by obedience to Christ?

- Discuss with a trusted friend your motivations for ministry: the 3 B's, personal comfort, pleasing Christ, other?

- Discuss with your church leadership this question: "How will our church fulfill the Great Commission for each of our concentric circles?" What is our next step?

- Read and study church planting in the book of Acts. List the sacrifices made for church multiplication.

- If you agree with the concepts in this chapter, preach a message or teach a lesson on the topic.

---

[1] Ralph Moore, *Starting a New Church; The Church Planter's Guide to Success* (Ventura, CA; Regal Books, 2002) p. 28.

[2] John F. Walvoord and Roy B. Zuck, eds., *The Bible Knowledge Commentary, New Testament* (Wheaton, IL: Victor Books, 1983), p. 409.

[3] From a conversation with Phil Stevenson in 2000.

[4] From a conversation with Jim Moss, East Pennsylvania Churches of God, General Conference, 1999.

Chapter 2

Three Laws of Reproduction

What comes to mind when you hear the word "evangelism?" Maybe you think of Billy Graham crusades or a home visitation ministry or special outreach events like Halloween alternative parties, Easter Egg hunts or Christian concerts. All of these efforts have their place. Some make for exciting and even sensational community events. But let's consider a better approach, the most biblical strategy.

When Barnabas and Saul left Antioch and intentionally began to obey Christ's Great Commission, what did they do? Studying the Book of Acts, we see that they used a simple strategy: they traveled from town to town, shared Jesus and started new churches. Soon they trained others to do the same.

Conclusion: There is no more biblical evangelistic strategy than planting churches.

That being the case, shouldn't we do what the apostles did? Planting new churches to reach people for Jesus, just as Christians did in Bible times is biblical and ageless.

Following the four gospel accounts of the life of Christ, the New Testament essentially tells the story of the planting and development of new churches. Acts chronicles the church planting journeys of Paul and others. The epistles give instruction on doctrinal and practical issues to new churches and pastors.

Even John's Revelation begins with instructions to seven of these churches. The Lord says,

> I will explain the mystery of the seven stars that you saw at my right side and the seven gold lampstands. The seven stars are the angels of the seven churches, and the lampstands are the seven churches. (Rev. 1:20, CEV)

Since each of these churches has an angel and a lampstand, perhaps this means that *every* church receives a guardian angel and a lampstand in heaven. Apparently, when we plant a church we light a lamp in heaven, as well as establish a "lighthouse" on earth. We can see that these seven churches, though flawed, were precious to the Lord.

Likewise, Jesus loves His churches today. Pastor Bill Hybels likes to say, "The church is the hope of the world." I think he means that God primarily uses the church for His work on earth—bringing people to Jesus and discipling them. I agree. Christ stated emphatically, "I will build my church; and the gates of hell shall not prevail against it" (Matt. 16:18b, KJV). Ephesians leaves no doubt about His feelings for his "bride;" "Christ loved the church and gave himself up for her" (Eph 5:25b, NIV).

We can't read the New Testament with an open mind and not conclude that God loves church planting! It is a "history book" on church planting, a "love letter" from the Groom to His Bride and a "handbook" for the nurture of healthy new churches. Therefore...

Law #1: The *most biblical* evangelistic methodology is church planting.

Some might object that church planting works best for areas that don't already have churches, but seems unnecessary for areas with many churches. We will address that objection more fully later. The fact remains that if we seriously pursue biblical evangelism, we must start with church planting and proceed from there.

I serve with Dynamic Church Planting International, a para-church ministry that trains leaders to plant churches all over the world. "Para" means called alongside. The local church holds preeminence as the most important ministry. Other ministries may come along side to help as needed.

Since Jesus loves His Church, He loves to see it multiplied to reach more lost people. Other outreach ministries may have more glitz and glamour for the Christian community and the public in general. But while they may get more "press," we should aim to please the Lord by pursuing biblical strategies, not what might serve to gain our own or others' approval.

THERE'S MORE

Yes, we should plant churches simply because it is the most biblical method of evangelism. But we have even more to motivate us. Not only is church planting the most biblical methodology for reaching our world, *it is also the most effective.*

I say this based on the research over the past two or three decades of missiologists and strategists, such as Dr. C. Peter Wagner, who concluded that, "The single most effective evangelistic methodology under heaven is planting new churches."[1]

What a statement! And others agree with Wagner. Renowned church researcher and prolific author Lyle Schaller writes,

> The most important single argument for making new church development a high priority is that this is the most effective means for reaching unchurched persons. Numerous studies have shown that *60 to 80 percent* of the new adult members of new congregations are persons who were not actively involved in the life of any worshipping congregations immediately prior to joining that new mission. By contrast, *most long established churches draw the majority of their new adult members from persons who transfer in from other congregations.*[2] (italics mine)

That is a remarkable statistic—60-80% new believers in each new church. Picture thousands of church plants of 50, 100, 200, 300, or 500 people with 60-80% new followers of Christ! See the tremendous spiritual harvest! If we start a hundred new churches and each results in an average of just a hundred conversions, they will produce 10,000 new believers. 1,000 new churches = 100,000 new believers. 10,000 = a million. One hundred new believers might be a conservative number—one of the daughter churches I was involved in has now seen almost 1,500 conversions! Thus,

Law #2: The *most effective* evangelistic methodology is church planting.

Furthermore, because those converts already connect with a follow up mechanism (the church), they usually become real disciples, not just registered "decisions" that may or may not signify real commitments to Christ.

Research based on worldwide data with a pool of 9,000 churches found that churches that have planted daughter churches are growing three times faster than those who haven't (47 per 100 over 5 years vs. 15 per 100 over 5 years). These figures include the members given away over these last five years.[3]

Want further proof of the evangelistic effectiveness of church planting? Then just visit new churches and listen to the testimonies of new believers. Or read on and enjoy more wonderful stories of conversions through church planting.

People like the Solis family. When we started our new church, they were unchurched and unsaved. We got to know Andres and Louise through their son's involvement in our son's Cub Scout troop. We invited them to church on Easter and they came. After a few weeks of church attendance, my wife Carolyn and I asked if we could show them how to know Christ personally. They said "yes" and when we visited them, all four chose to follow Christ: Andres, Louise, Nick and Grandmother Eva. Since then they have been walking with Christ and serving in that church.

New churches abound with stories such as this. If you like reading this, just think how God feels! Jesus said in Luke 15:7, "I tell you that in the same way there will be more rejoicing in heaven over one sinner who repents than over ninety-nine righteous persons who do not need to repent" (NIV).

Can you imagine the parties in heaven when new churches start and people are saved? How do angels celebrate? Perhaps with singing, shouting, blowing trumpets, doing back flips on clouds, giving high-fives with their angel wings, eating angel food cake… Whatever they do, I'm sure it is exuberant.

We must plant churches to reach new people for Christ, not to "reshuffle the deck" of believers in our town. God wants us to plant churches to bring lost people to salvation by the most effective methodology.

People often ask, "Why are they so effective?" Sometimes those asking attend established churches in evangelistic stagnation and numerical decline. I can hear their frustration and pain as they wonder, "Why do new churches reach so many people when our own church struggles to reach a few souls for Christ. Is there something wrong with us?"

I see five main reasons for the evangelistic effectiveness of new churches:

1. Cause Orientation. Most new churches start with few people, no buildings, limited programs and few resources. But they have something that money can't buy: a passionate commitment to a cause. The church planting team embarks on a quest to take a town or region for Jesus, to snatch lost people from the grip of hell, to build a disciple-making church.

What kinds of people start churches? Visionaries, risk takers, pioneers. What drives them to take the risks and pay the price? The vision of reaching people for Jesus and building His church. If you asked them, most would say that the benefits far outweigh the cost they pay to win the lost.

2. Survival. If a new church does not grow, in most cases it won't survive. Maybe not a noble motivation, but certainly compelling. The average church plant starts with a handful of people. They would like to eventually afford to adequately support their pastor, own a building, support missions, build a youth ministry, and so on. Those things won't happen until the church becomes financially viable. These goals motivate them to grow.

As a church planter in my late 20's, I was highly motivated to feed and house my family. My wife liked that idea too! Now, don't get me wrong. I truly wanted to spread the Gospel—the cause. But my financial obligations and our church goals lent urgency to our mission. We needed to grow, we HAD to grow, or we would not survive.

3. Adaptability. Most established churches gear their ministry to serve their own constituency, their congregation of the converted. Inadvertently, they sometimes erect barriers to reaching lost people. They might use:

- Strange and incomprehensible language and terminology (sanctification, washed in the blood, propitiation, redeemed, eschatology, dispensation, etc.),

- Incomprehensible versions of the Bible (thee, thou, sayest, knowest, becometh, whoremonger, brimstone, abomination, pertaineth),

- Outdated styles of music (organ music, hymns with strange words and phrases),

- And uncomfortable mindsets (judgmentalism, "offensive" political stances, etc.).

Some churches relish this tendency, such as a church I found on the Internet, which advertised, "Berean Grace Church: a church for Bible believers, preaching grace in the dispensation of grace." Most lost people would not understand the point of that ad—written in a foreign language: "Christianeze." While not so blatant, most established churches have at least a similar mindset: we exist to serve our members plus those believers out there just like us who agree with the way we do things.

The apostle and church planter Paul had a different attitude, the attitude usually predominant in new churches. He said, "I have become **all** things to **all** men so that by **all** possible means I might save some" (1 Corinthians 9:22b—emphasis mine). Paul was willing to do anything he could, within biblical parameters, to reach lost people more effectively.

Usually people in established churches bear no conscious malice in their reluctance to relate to lost people. They simply can't see cultural dinosaurs lurking behind their mantra, "We've always done it that way."

Once I spoke at an adult Sunday school class in the church I grew up in. The teacher asked me to speak about barriers to church growth. I shared an example using the second verse of the great hymn "Come Thou Fount," which contains the line, "here I raise mine Ebenezer." I asked the class what this line meant. No one knew. This illustrated my point about singing songs that even Christians didn't understand, let alone lost people. As "luck" would have it, in the church service that followed, we sang "Come Thou Fount!" I wonder if they will make the effort to translate "Christianeze" for the lost people who might wander into a future service.

4. Attraction. Usually, when established Christians want a new church, they look for an established congregation with church amenities they have come to expect. A flourishing youth ministry. Comfy seats that don't require set up or take down before and after church. An attractive building. An opportunity to join a thriving ministry. And so on. Most shy away from a new church startup that features few of these comforts.

But lost people often do not know to look for all these amenities. They just search for answers to life issues: who am I, what am I here for, where am I going, how can I have peace with God? When new churches answer those questions, it does not matter whatever else they lack—they provide Jesus.

For new churches to grow, they must reach lost people because established Christians generally hesitate to join. This forces the new church to grow via evangelism instead of transfer growth.

5. The Nature of Life. We humans can't escape the fact that our physical growth happens in our youth. When we become adults, we stop growing physically. Ultimately, we grow old and die. Like it or not. The same cycle applies to churches. Like people, churches tend to experience their biggest growth spurt early in their history and then stop growing. Most churches plateau at a certain size. They usually find it extremely difficult to grow bigger after a long plateau, especially after they become accustomed to that size. A few churches last as long as the oldest trees on earth—a thousand years or more. However, even those exceptions to the rule eventually disband. Generally, churches follow the life cycle of birth, growth, plateau, stagnation and eventual death.

How can churches overcome this life cycle? The best way is to *become a mother church by giving life to daughter churches*. This way, life continues on and on. While the mother church may grow frail and die, vigorous life continues on in the legacy of daughter churches, granddaughter churches, great granddaughter churches and so on.

Am I opposed to established churches? Of course not—I hope all new churches become established. However, we must recognize that gradually, in the natural course of events, most churches will tend to focus inwardly on meeting the needs of their constituents, which will decrease their vision and capability to reach the lost.

That's why new churches remain the most effective method of evangelism and why we should utilize this God-given method to reach the world with the Good News of Jesus. Now let's consider another question.

SO, HOW CAN WE BEST PLANT CHURCHES?

Law #3: The *most natural and effective* way to start churches is daughter church planting.

This statement deserves a lot of explanation.

First, why do we call it "daughter" church planting? The church, as the bride of Christ, is female, so we use the feminine gender when we refer to churches. That makes for "sister" churches instead of "brother" churches. "Mother" churches give birth to "daughter" churches.

Let's look at three reasons why the most natural and effective way to plant churches is by mother-daughter church planting.

1. Conception. Nowadays, we can conceive a child in a Petri dish and produce a "test tube baby." But, that's not the natural way to conceive a child. Likewise, a denomination or association of churches can begin a church. However, a local church, the bride of Christ, can more naturally conceive and then birth the daughter.

I believe God desires this, and it follows the natural order of His creation. Like begets like. Sheep beget sheep—not shepherds! Cows beget cows—not mice. Turtles beget turtles. Dogs beget dogs. Likewise,

1. Christians should beget Christians. (Not pastors/shepherds or churches)

2. Churches should beget churches. (Not denominations—although they should play a vital role as the "doctors and nurses" that assist in the delivery of baby churches.)

3. Associations should beget associations. (We hope that so many churches beget churches that it becomes necessary to multiply associational regions!)

Daughter church planting holds far greater potential for multiplication than church planting initiated by denominations. Consider the numbers. The USA has about 350,000 churches now. If only half of them daughter a new church, that would add 175,000 new churches. A great evangelistic movement would surely sweep our land—based on the information we have seen in the two axioms above.

Now let's look at the denominations in the US, currently numbering 200?[4] If every denomination planted *ten* churches, that would add only 2,000 new churches reaching lost people with the Gospel. Even planting a hundred each would add only 20,000 new churches.

We need denominational groups to assist the local church, not to replace it in its role of church planting. Yet too many pastors and church leaders seem to think that they should leave church planting to their denomination.

Christian Schwarz makes this observation in his book, *Natural Church Development*:

Hardly anything demonstrates the health of a congregation as much as the willingness—and ability!—to give birth to new congregations. The opposite is true as well. Hardly anything is a more clear indication of illness than structures, which by design hinder church multiplication, or at best permit it as an absolute exception.[5]

Plain and simple, a healthy church reproduces. It is the natural way to conceive and reproduce healthy churches.

2. Nurturing. Churches should reproduce by daughtering because baby churches need nurturing. Like human babies, baby churches need a mother to love and care for them. Imagine newborn children without a mom. Our hearts go out to such children. We place them in orphanages, in foster homes, or up for adoption because they need someone to take care of them. Our society arrests and prosecutes mothers who abandon their children. Yet, we allow churches to start without the nurture of a loving mother.

A mother church can provide nurture by furnishing:

• Encouragement and support when things get difficult.

• A place to celebrate when things go well.

• A family to help care for needs that may arise.

• Wise counsel in the strategic decisions of church life.

• Discipline when appropriate.

3. Resources. Carolyn and I have three sons. One day when our oldest was nineteen, I walked through his bedroom and it struck me that because of his youth he had virtually nothing. The sum of his earthly possessions consisted of a CD player, a skateboard, a bicycle, some books, some papers, clothes and a video game. I, on the other hand, own a home, have a job, a car to drive, household furnishings and some savings. Compared to my son, I'm well off, simply because I have had time to get established in life.

Now I don't believe I must provide for my sons forever, but I should share with them to get them started in life. I don't have a whole lot, but I have far more than they do. I can help them get a college education, buy their first car, someday help them with a wedding, and maybe even help them buy a home. Probably they could make it without any help from me, but the things I provide can give them a great boost in life.

Likewise, a new church benefits immensely when a mother church provides some basic resources to get started in life such as:

- Leaders and workers (long term or short term)
- Facilities
- Oversight
- Site selection assistance
- Training
- Promotion
- Representation
- Finances

Usually the more resources a new church has to start with, the more successful the church will become.[6]

Notice that money comes at the end of this list. I did that on purpose. The most important resource that a mother church can provide is people. People bring leadership, service, prayer, bodies to fill chairs and greet people and finances as well. All of these resources give the new church a good start in life.

CHAPTER SUMMARY

In this chapter we have seen three laws of reproduction that produce the greatest possible evangelistic harvest in God's Kingdom:

Law #1: The *most biblical* evangelistic methodology is church planting.

Law #2: The *most effective* evangelistic methodology is church planting.

Law #3: The *most natural and effective* way to start churches is daughter church planting.

You now have a choice: get involved or sit on the sidelines. Why sit by when so much is at stake?

Prayer Points: How you can pray about the concepts in this chapter:

- Pray that pastors and church leaders across your nation recognize that the most biblical and most effective method of evangelism is church planting.

- Pray that Christians will see daughter church planting as the best way to start churches and want to get involved.

- Pray that God will raise up church planting pastors and teams.

- Pray that nothing would hinder the realization of this vision.

Action Steps: What you can do to begin to implement the steps in this chapter.

- Discuss the three axioms with leaders in your church.
- Study Paul's declaration of evangelistic pragmatism in 1 Corinthians 9:19-27. Then study the sacrifice Timothy made to make this happen in Acts 16:1-3.

- Rate your church's receptivity to planting a daughter church: very high, high, mild, indifferent, opposed, highly opposed.

- If you agree strongly with these three laws, preach a message or teach a lesson on the topic.

Chapter 3

The Joys of Parenting

We were two weeks into our first church plant. Carolyn "promised" she would not have our baby on Sunday morning. But sure enough, Sunday morning September 13, 1981, after a quick call to a friend to fill the pulpit for me, we headed to the hospital for the birth of our first son, Gabriel Mark Williams. Gabriel means "man of God."

I couldn't have been more proud to be a parent. Over the years, we have had the wonderful experience of parenting Gabe, and later, Danny and Benjamin. Ask any group of parents what they love most and usually their children will top the list. Almost nothing brings us as much joy and satisfaction as our kids.

Likewise, being the parent of daughter churches brings tremendous joy. Pastors of mother churches often tell me of their pride and delight over their daughter churches. I feel the same way about mine. Just as God made us to love parenting children He created the same joy for the church.

Let's consider some of the awesome joys of parenting churches:

1. Watching your "Children" Grow Up and Succeed. In the early 1990's, Paul Becker brought Hal and Lori Seed to our home to talk about planting a church in the area. They wondered if I would consider helping to "daughter" a new church.

My prayers confirmed that the Lord wanted us to help them in any way we could. After they moved to town, I helped Hal contact people in our church to recruit them for his core team. Eventually about 15 people, almost 10 percent of our congregation, went to help start New Song Community Church in nearby Oceanside, California. While still the senior pastor in the mother church, I served as the chair of the new church's board for three years.

We gave birth to a big fat baby "daughter," weighing in at almost 200 people the first day. "She" began to grow. I watched her baby steps with pride. Occasionally she suffered bumps and bruises, but we encouraged our offspring to keep going, despite the growth pains. I watched with joy as she celebrated her first birthday.

New Song consistently reached lost people with the Good News and I had the joy of hearing the wonderful testimonies. In three years or so, she "graduated" to become completely self-supporting. Later she moved to her first "apartment" when New Song leased a facility. New Song bought a first home when she was about eight years old.

Within ten years, New Song had grown to about 800 people in worship each weekend and "daughtered" three other churches. Best of all, the ministry of these four churches had seen over 1,300 people profess faith in Jesus Christ.

Like most parents, I am immensely proud of my daughter church and the other churches we birthed. They are some of the very greatest joys of my ministry. When I look back at what we accomplished in our church, virtually nothing stands out as much as giving birth to these "children." Many people will be in heaven because of them. I feel like Paul when he wrote to the church in Philippi, "I thank my God every time I remember you" (Phil 1:3, NIV).

2. Causing Family Growth. It doesn't occur to many Christians to wonder, "Where do baby churches come from?" Like small children who assume that babies just magically appear, they seem to think that baby churches just happen.

Eventually, children begin to wonder about babies. Hopefully, they come to understand that children are the natural, normal result of a loving marriage between a husband and a wife. Likewise, a love relationship between Christ the Groom and His Bride the Church *should* result in baby churches.

What if God had not placed within us the desire to reproduce? The human race would die out. Without offspring we would become extinct within one generation.

Likewise, God designed churches to reproduce. If churches do not reproduce, the Family of God will gradually shrink resulting eventually in church extinction.

However, if churches reproduce, the Family of God increases. The more they reproduce, the greater the increase. Fewer churches mean Family decline. More churches mean Family expansion.

3. Creating Ministry Flow to Avoid Stagnation and Stench. Guajome Lake lies just off Route 76, near our home in Southern California. Guajome is an American Indian word meaning "frog pond." Our family has enjoyed this beautiful little lake many times.

However, in late summer, this pleasant area can stink to high heaven. For a long time I couldn't figure out why. What could cause such a lovely lake to become so foul? One day I asked a park ranger. He said that the smell comes from oxygen depletion. In the spring, the lake fills from a river fed by snow melt off a nearby mountain. But by summertime the river dries up trapping water in the lake and forcing the fish to rely on the oxygen in the remaining stagnant water. As the oxygen depletes, the fish die. They float to the surface and rot. Rotting fish really stink.

Similarly, without a flow of ministry through a church, it tends to stagnate, rot and stink. It must have an outlet lest it becomes ingrown, self-centered, selfish and smelly. Far too many Christians go to church and just "sit, soak and sour."

Or to change the analogy, unless we let the sheep out of the pen, the sheep dung piles up too high! Luis Palau said it this way, "The church is like manure: pile it up and it stinks up the neighborhood, spread it out and it enriches the world." Even if you think this analogy "stinks," it conveys an obvious truth—Christians must spread themselves out to bless the world and one of the very best ways to do that is to send people out to do daughter church planting.

4. Receiving the Blessing God Gives to Givers. As a local church pastor, I wanted people to give to the Lord through our church. I happily pointed out that the Bible promises rewards for those who give. Eventually I realized, with the help of some godly church members, that He would also bless churches that give. Therefore, in my second church plant we tithed its offerings to missions from the very first day. God honored that giving with financial prosperity and many other rewards.

Maybe you have experienced the same thing in your life and church. If so, I would like to challenge you to another level. God also blesses when we "tithe" a different kind of gift: people. The first church I planted "gave" about 10 percent of our congregation to plant New Song Church. Frankly, it was one of the biggest sacrifices I've ever made—we gave some of our best people. However, it was also one of the best things I ever did. When I see the fruit that came to New Song, I am extremely glad we "gave" those people and that they willingly became "missionaries" to our own backyard. Furthermore, since the church was so close, we had no trouble finding out what happened with our "gift." We watched as the return on investment grew and grew.

5. Seeing Miracles of God's Provision. Some church leaders think they cannot birth a daughter church because they don't have enough resources. On the contrary, that is a tremendous reason FOR starting a daughter church. Why? Because when we do something beyond our own resources – simply because it is God's desire – then we get to watch Him do miracle after miracle of provision that turn it into a reality.

When was the last time you trusted God for something you knew would only happen if He came through for you? What keeps you from stepping onto the ragged edge of faith? After all, "Without faith it is impossible to please God" (Hebrews 11:6a). What have you done lately to exercise faith in God? When was the last time you really launched out to do His will, trusting that He would provide? As someone said, "Why not go out on a limb, that's where the fruit is."

Stories abound of churches that sent a significant number from their congregation to start a daughter church and God miraculously sent replacement people by the next Sunday. Similar stories tell of miraculous financial provision from the Lord.

Am I promising a miracle every time? Obviously I cannot do that. However, the Scripture promises, "And my God will meet all your needs according to his glorious riches in Christ Jesus" (Phil 4:19, NIV).

6. Reaching People Groups Your Church Cannot Reach. As a pastor, I wanted to reach everyone in my area with the Good News of Christ. However, I had a problem. Some people in our community did not speak English, only Spanish or Japanese, and I did not speak either. What could I do? Ignore them? No! Hope they would learn English someday? Certainly not! They needed a ministry in their own language. Thankfully, some believers who spoke those languages started churches and we agreed to partner with them.

While language is the most obvious barrier to reaching people, other barriers keep churches from effectively reaching people in their neighborhoods. For instance, incredible as it may seem, not everyone thought I was the most wonderful pastor they had ever met. Some actually tried my church and then joined another church. Others tried our church but left and never connected with it or any other church. Of course, the same thing happens in your community.

Different personalities, looks, accents, ministry styles, and even styles of humor appeal to different people. The look of the building, the type of music, the location, the associate staff, the "personality" of the church, the length of the services and many other issues can attract or repel people. Pastor Rick Warren commented, "It takes all kinds of churches to reach all kinds of people." Therefore, more options create more potential for finding a church that fits individual needs and preferences.

It takes a certain level of maturity to admit that "my" church doesn't appeal to everyone. Does that end our obligation? Do we simply write them off and forget them?

No, we must not overlook them. God wants lost people found. Jesus said, "I tell you that in the same way there will be more rejoicing in heaven over one sinner who repents than over ninety-nine righteous persons who do not need to repent" (Luke 15:7, NIV). Jesus stated His life purpose in Luke 19:10, "For the Son of Man came to seek and to save what was lost." "Jesus answered them, 'It is not the healthy who need a doctor, but the sick. I have not come to call the righteous, but sinners to repentance'" (Luke 5:31-32, NIV).

Taking a territory for Christ requires multiple churches. One of the biggest joys of parenting a church comes when you see your daughter church reach people that you could not have reached. Why become intimidated or offended by this truth? God wants us to rejoice in the fact that others can reach people we cannot.

7. Leaving a Family Legacy. As living organisms, churches have a life span. Some churches live briefly and some live for many, many years. But all die eventually. The majority of the church planting efforts recorded in the Acts of the Apostles occurred in Turkey. Those churches died long ago. In fact, today Turkey is 99.8% Muslim.

Usually pastors and people in thriving churches don't see the dying churches. We don't want to. Nevertheless, those in denominational leadership deal with the many churches that pass away each year. They know only too well that we must plant churches just to replace the ones that die.

Will your church leave a legacy of churches when it passes away some day? I hope so.

A pastor described a funeral service for a church as the most beautiful church service he ever attended. For some reason the New York City church decided to close its doors for good. People gathered time from all the churches birthed out of that prolific church, representing daughters, granddaughters, even great-granddaughter churches. They celebrated the life of a wonderful mother church.

I want the same legacy of offspring for my church and for yours.

8. Increasing Evangelistic Passion in the Mother Church. A wonderful evangelistic awakening often happens when a church becomes a mother. As the baby church reaches out to the lost and wins people to Christ, the mother church gets infected with an "evangelistic bug" and asks, "Why can't the same thing happen here?" Desire increases. People pray more for the lost. She tries new strategies she learns from the daughter church. And both churches win people to Jesus.

9. Developing New Leadership. Many churches hesitate to plant a daughter church for fear of losing leaders. However, God rewards churches that share leaders by developing new leadership in both the mother and daughter churches.

Think about what happens in our bodies when we donate blood. Do we lose it forever? No, God designed the body so that it replaces blood loss.

In the same way, God designed the body of Christ so that when we donate the "lifeblood" of key leaders, the body replaces the leaders. Many times this happens through people who have been sitting on the sidelines without participating in ministry. Maybe they thought that they weren't needed. Other times God brings in new blood—either mature Christians who join our church or new converts who become leaders. Trust him—the Great Physician knows how to care for his own Body!

The daughter church also develops new leadership. When Dan and Debby Proctor left my first church plant to help start the second, neither had been involved in any ministry. Nevertheless, because the new church plant needed them, they emerged as key leaders. After gaining four years of experience, they helped start one of the granddaughter churches. Eventually, Dan joined our staff at Dynamic Church Planting International as a full-time missionary. Why did Dan and Debby become leaders? Because of the need in the daughter church—church planting develops leaders.

10. Growing by Multiplication. I believe that the Apostle Paul had the greatest ministry of any New Testament leader other than Jesus Christ. But, how would he measure up against the standard of many modern church leaders who consider megachurches as the pinnacle of success? By that standard, Paul was a failure. Usually, his churches were small and struggling. None of them had their own buildings. Most just scraped by financially. Yet Paul's ministry had immense Kingdom impact because he planted churches that planted churches, resulting in church multiplication.

Is everyone called to be an itinerant church planter like Paul? No. Yet God calls every Christian to help spread the Gospel as effectively as possible. That means church multiplication.

Picture again the choice confronting the church in Antioch of Syria. Acts 13 tells us that the Holy Spirit told them to set apart Barnabas and Saul as missionary church planters. Did they relish the thought of having Barnabas and Saul leave their fellowship? I sincerely doubt it. They loved these two great leaders, Paul the incredible teacher and Barnabas the tremendous encourager. Even if Paul maybe annoyed them sometimes, they must have cherished Barnabas and his loving encouragement.

Nevertheless, they set aside their desire for fellowship to pursue the spread of the Gospel. They sent their two key leaders and the Gospel spread west to the rest of Asia, westward into Europe, and eventually to the New World.

What if they had squelched that vision? What if they decided to grow the church in Antioch as large as they could? What if they had said things like:
- "Now is not the time,"
- "We can't afford it,"
- "We can't spare the leadership,"
- "The persecution is too intense," and so on?

Now picture that church as they gathered to hear the missionary reports from Barnabas and Saul when they returned from their journeys. How do you think they felt? I'm convinced that their hearts bubbled over with praise and joy over the multiplication of churches and the spread of the Gospel. I believe God wants that for every church.

11. Sharing the Load. Call me a sissy if you want, but I want to share the responsibility for the spread of the Gospel. I do not want to carry the entire responsibility.

The church I founded in 1981 eventually became the mother, grandmother or partner church for six other churches, all within a fifteen minute driving distance from one another in Northern San Diego County. They work together to reach the lost. Far from being saturated with churches, this area needs dozens more churches. No one church can do the job. No one church should want to try to do it alone. We must share the load.

In Exodus 18 Moses learned to share the load. He had tried to judge all the Israelites' disputes himself, and it overburdened him. Relief came when he found associates to help him. Furthermore, the people received better care.

Likewise, we have a responsibility to evangelize our area, but we need help. Relief comes when we plant daughter churches to assist in evangelizing our area.

12. Producing a Bigger "Bottom-line." Many people like to get to the bottom of an issue. I certainly do. In ministry, the bottom line is glorifying Jesus through the growing His Kingdom. Jesus gave us a mandate to, "Go and make disciples" (Matt 28:19). We must do all we can to help make that happen.

The chart below outlines the bottom line results from my daughter church planting efforts, thus far. The church at the top, Emmanuel Baptist, is the mother, grandmother or partner church for all the others in the table. Notice the most important number, not the attendance at Emmanuel Baptist, but the total attendance at the bottom of the chart.

Emmanuel Baptist Church Family Tree
Easter attendance, an easy and exciting day to "number the people!"

NAME	BIRTH	RELATIONSHIP	STYLE	1999	2000
Emmanuel Baptist Church	8/23/81	Founding Pastor	Semi-Traditional	140	151
Iglesia Camino Real	1/88	Partner	Spanish	112	110?
Lake Tulloch Bible Church	4/23/91	Daughter	Independant Charismatic	350	400
New Song Church	9/27/92	Daughter	Willow, Boomer	1,003	1,253
Japanese Christian Church of Vista	7/10/94	Partner	Japanese American	65	40
New Hope Church	10/4/94	Founding Pastor	Seeker Sensitive	375	400
Rock Springs Church	10/4/98	Granddaughter	Buster	71	109
Iglesia Christian Emmanuel	2/21/99	Granddaughter	Spanish	50	100
TOTALS "The Bottom Line"				**2,166**	**2,563**

See how much we can multiply Kingdom impact through daughter church planting? Sure, I wish the numbers were bigger. But I'm thankful that at least we did not just settle for one church. The "bottom line" grows because of our parenting efforts.

Let me ask you this: What if we had chosen to start only one church? We might have grown the church a bit larger, but I know we would not have been at the 2,500 level, the bottom line of all these churches.

Leaders who think bottom line must think about the power of church multiplication and their "family tree." Many who read this book will grow a "family tree" far larger than this, for which heaven rejoices and I say "amen!"

13. Pleasing my Commanding Officer. As a child, whenever we could request hymns in our church, I would ask for "Onward Christian Soldiers." The military march style of music, plus the battle theme of the lyrics, captured my boyish heart.

Today we often lose sight of the fact that we have a war against evil we must win as soldiers in the Lord's army. We should aim to please our Commander. "No one serving as a soldier gets involved in civilian affairs – he wants to please his commanding officer" (2 Timothy 2:4).

When we plant daughter churches to reach the lost, we can rest secure knowing that we please our Commanding Officer. Nothing should bring us greater joy.

CHAPTER SUMMARY

In this chapter, we examined thirteen reasons that make parenting a joyful experience. Like the human experience, the blessings far outweigh the cost. Some benefits appear immediately and some will come in Glory. Best of all, we put a smile on the face of the Lord Jesus.

Prayer Points: How you can pray about the concepts in this chapter:

- Pray that the Lord multiplies the joys of mother churches.
- Pray that daughter churches thrive to produce a huge return on the investment.
- Pray that church leaders focus on the joys of parenting instead of the costs.
- Pray that pastors lead their churches toward parenting.

Action Steps: What you can do to begin to implement the steps in this chapter.

- Study the points in this chapter.
- Add any other joys of parenting that come to mind.
- On a scale of one to ten, rate the importance of each of the joys discussed in this chapter. Review your results with other leaders in your church
- If you agree strongly about the joys of daughter church planting, preach a message or teach a lesson on the topic.

---

[1] C. Peter Wagner, *Church Planting for a Greater Harvest* (Ventura, CA: Regal Books, 1990), p. 11.

[2] Lyle Schaller, "Why Start New Churches?" *The Circuit Rider*, May 1979, p. 3.

[3] From the Institute for Natural Church Development International, www.ncd-international.org. "Honestly," says Christoph Schalk, "the question of how to do the calculation with reference to the members given away is a little tricky and it is still being studied, but even if we remove the members 'given away' from the mother churches' growth, they are still slightly better off in terms of growth speed than the sterile churches: 17 per 100 over 5 years as opposed to 15 per 100 over 5 years. But I'm not sure that calculating things this way is really fair to the mother churches. What we also need to begin studying are the growth rates of the daughter churches."

Church growth is not the only benefit of planting churches. A positive correlation was also found between church health and planting daughter churches. As measured by the NCD survey, the composite health level of the mother churches was 5 points better than that of the sterile churches: 53 vs. 48.

[4] Eileen W. Lindner, ed. *Yearbook of American & Canadian Churches* (Nashville: Abingdon, 1999), p. 170-172.

[5] Christian Schwarz, *Natural Church Development* (Carol Stream, IL: ChurchSmart Resources, 1996), p. 69.

[6] An exception to this might be when a megachurch provides so many people that the new church becomes inwardly focused instead of outreach focused.

Chapter 4

God Loves Big Families

My brother Brian and his wonderful wife Judy have taken seriously God's directive to "multiply and replenish the earth" by having eleven children. Large families aren't the norm now in the United States. When people ask me, "What is their problem?" I explain that they just love children. It is not a problem; they are a wonderful Christian family.

What *is* a problem is when churches fail to reproduce themselves. That's because, ever since the Book of Acts, the Gospel spread as believers shared Jesus and planted churches and those churches planted churches. They longed to saturate the world with the Gospel. When this happens, societies change.

Eddie Gibbs has described the early church as spreading like a strawberry patch. When a strawberry plant begins to grow and produce fruit, it does not stop with just one plant and a few berries. It sends out runners, which also send down roots, begin a new plant and produce fruit. Each of these plants sends out runners of their own that create more plants and produce more fruit. Soon an area is covered with a network of strawberry plants, called a strawberry patch.

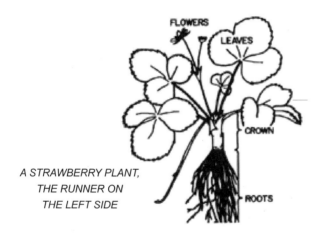

A STRAWBERRY PLANT, THE RUNNER ON THE LEFT SIDE

IT IS FUN TO HARVEST A STRAWBERRY PATCH!

My grandparents cultivated a big strawberry patch on their farm in Northern Michigan. Grandma would make the most delicious strawberry shortcake.

Perhaps strawberries don't grow where you live. Our friend Dr. Jayakumar of Bangalore, India, pointed out that banyan trees also send down runners or branches that increase the size of the tree by creating roots and forming a new section of the tree. The famous Big Banyan Tree sprawls over almost three acres of land near his home!

THE AUTHOR BY A BIG BANYAN TREE

Much like strawberry plants or banyan trees, the early church constantly sprouted new organisms—new churches. They didn't aim just to have one big congregation and build bigger and better buildings and offerings. The early church didn't even have church buildings, they met in homes. Instead, they aimed to convert their city, region, and, indeed, the whole world. To achieve that goal, they knew they had to blanket their area with churches. Like the house church movement in China today, they thrived through spreading a network of reproductive churches even though they faced persecution.

Please do not misunderstand; I'm not against large churches. In fact, I hope your church grows much larger, while planting daughter churches. The objective of daughter church planting should not be to limit the size of the mother. Some churches have said, "We only want to grow to X size, and then plant daughter churches to keep us from growing." In fact, that approach often doesn't work—the mother church plants daughters and still keeps growing. The best objective is to reach as many people as possible with the Good News in BOTH the mother and daughter churches.

Pastor Rick Warren, the well-known author of *The Purpose Driven Life*, comments that, "The mark of a truly mature church is that it has babies: It starts other churches. You do not have to be a large church to start new congregations. Saddleback Church started our first daughter church when our church was just a year old. Each year since then we've started at least one new daughter church."[1]

As the founding pastor of one of the largest churches in the USA, Pastor Warren wisely realizes that even his mega-church cannot reach all the people in his region. Their daughter churches will reach folks nearby that he could never reach in his church. No wonder God has blessed him so much.

I've been pleased to find this multiplication mindset among many African pastors. They consider planting daughter churches a prime responsibility for any church. Typically when I ask a younger African pastor, "Have you started any daughter churches?" he will respond with something like, "Only three, but we are planning to start many more." Often longer established pastors have planted 20, 30, 50 and even more daughter churches.

In the US, many of our churches seem intent on growing the biggest strawberry in the world. I've seen some big strawberries in my time, but they were still only bite sized. The biggest strawberry ever can't compare to thousands of strawberries in a strawberry patch. We don't need big strawberry churches as much as we need strawberry patches of churches that together reach the world for Christ.

EXCITING CHURCH PLANTING MOVEMENTS

David Garrison has written about some of the greatest contemporary church planting "strawberry patches" in the world, which he calls "Church Planting Movements." He defines a Church Planting Movement as, "a rapid multiplication of indigenous churches planting churches that sweeps through a people group or population segment."[2]

Garrison cites thrilling instances of church planting movements. For example:

❖ In India, over 4,000 new churches and some 300,000 new believers among Bhojpuri-speaking peoples;[3]

❖ In Southern China, over 90,000 baptized believers in 920 house churches in eight years time;[4]

❖ Cambodia saw over 60,000 new Christians and hundreds of new churches planted in ten years;[5]

❖ 13,000 Kazakh conversions over a decade and a half.[6]

God does awesome works when His people are willing to plant churches!

Many of these Church Planting Movements are composed of house churches that can range from around ten people up to as many as 85.[7] Some are *house churches* and others are *cell churches*. What's the difference between the two? Garrison explains, "*House churches* are stand-alone churches that happen to be small enough to meet in homes. After filling their limited space, they grow through multiplication rather than increasing their membership. Each house church has its own leadership and derives its authority directly from Christ, rather than through a hierarchy, and functions in every way as a church."[8]

He continues, "*Cell churches*, on the other hand, are actually large churches that have organized their membership into small cell groups that are not self-consciously functioning as independent churches. Cell churches derive their authority from a senior pastor whose teaching cascades down to each cell group leader. Like house churches, cell churches may grow through multiplication, but they never break ties with the centralized leadership."[9]

HOW SHOULD WE DEFINE "CHURCH"?

Do house churches qualify as true, biblical churches? What basic requirements must we meet before we call something a church? At the very least, it must meet the standard of Matthew 18:20 (KJV). "When two or three are gathered in my name, there am I in the midst." Using this passage, Gene Getz writes, "I personally tend toward a simple definition: a body of believers can be called a church whenever that group meets together regularly for mutual edification."[10] I know of others who also feel that this is an adequate definition.

It seems risky to hang a definition of something as crucial as *church* on one verse, especially one that, in context, is addressing church discipline, which is just one aspect of a healthy church. Proper rules of Bible interpretation (hermeneutics) would suggest that we draw a fuller definition that includes all the relevant Bible passages that describe the church. So I suggest this short definition:

> *A church is a group of born again believers in Christ who meet regularly for biblical worship and are led by shepherds who preach the Word and lead the congregation toward the purpose of glorifying God by fulfilling Jesus' Great Commission and Greatest Commandments.*

Let's unpack this definition:

❖ *A church*: Sometimes the Greek word translated "church" (*ekklesia*) refers to the universal church (all born again believers), but more commonly it refers to a local church, which is my meaning.

❖ *is a group of born again believers*: This distinguishes the true church from groups and cults that can wrongly label themselves a "church."

❖ *who meet regularly for biblical worship*: Usually this means meeting at least weekly to practice such things as singing, prayer, the Ordinances, exhorting and encouraging each other, giving and other forms of worship, and exercising spiritual gifts.

❖ *are led by shepherds*: The Greek word POIMEN, usually translated "pastor," literally means "shepherd." These leaders are more commonly called "elders" (PRESBUTEROS) signifying leaders with mature spiritual experience. A third Greek word used of the same office is EPISCOPOS which signifies managing or overseeing the manpower, money, gifts of the Spirit and other resources for the good of the church. In the New Testament, the term "elder," is always plural except for two times when it refers to the office of elder. It wasn't until the second century that some churches had a single elder/shepherd.[11] "The consistent New Testament pattern is a plurality of elders."[12] Typically, a primary elder/shepherd leads a team of other lay and/or professional elders/shepherds who provide advice, partnership and accountability for each other. While not all churches in Bible times paid their professional elders/shepherds enough to live on and sometimes leaders like Paul had to become "tentmakers" by earning their living in other ways, a church is charged with adequate compensation of its staff elders/shepherds (1 Timothy 5:17-18; 1 Corinthians 9:14b).

❖ *who preach the Word and lead the congregation*: Shepherds/elders, like Timothy, must "preach the Word," according to 2 Timothy 4:2. Usually there is one primary teaching and leading shepherds/elder (1 Tim 5:17) and others who are "able to teach" (1 Tim 3:2) but who handle other ministry responsibilities and assist in leadership (Hebrews 13:17, 1 Thes. 5:12-13). Part of their leadership was to provide protection for the church through the correction of church discipline, (Matthew 18:15-17; 1 Cor 5:4-7, 11-13; 2 Tim 4:2; Titus 2:15, 3:10; 1 Peter 5:2).

❖ *toward the purpose of glorifying God by fulfilling Jesus' Great Commission*: Every believer and every church should "...go and make disciples..." (Matthew 28:19-20). Thus, the church's objective is to spread to all people the joy of knowing and serving Christ.

❖ *and Greatest Commandments*: "'Love the Lord your God with all your heart and with all your soul and with all your mind.' This is the first and greatest commandment. And the second is like it: 'Love your neighbor as yourself.' All the Law and the Prophets hang on these two commandments" (Matthew 22:37-40). That being so, every church should seek to obey His Great Commandments.

In my opinion, before labeling a cell group, home fellowship, home Bible study, prayer meeting, informal gathering, coffee clutch, accountability group, support group, or any other kind of gathering a "church," we need to examine it in the light of Scriptural qualifications, such as those above. Does a group meet these minimal requirements? If so, we can call it a church. If not, let's be careful of calling any Christian gathering a local church.

Notice also what we left out of this definition: a church building, a choir, a denominational affiliation, stained glass, a traditional Sunday School program, a Sunday bulletin, incorporation through a constitution and by-laws. Many of these might prove helpful, but they are not integral to a BIBLICAL definition of church and therefore they are optional.

WHAT ABOUT SEMINARY EDUCATION?

Many churches look for pastors who are "college educated, seminary graduated and ordained." Personally, I feel that if all possible, these are valuable qualifications that benefit the local church. But they are not always possible in all situations, times and locations around the world.

The vital issue is to be "biblically qualified." First Timothy 3 and Titus 1 clearly define the qualifications for an elder/ pastor. While certainly beneficial, college and seminary education and ordination are not biblical mandates. But the qualifications listed in 1 Timothy and Titus *are* biblical mandates. Some churches may prefer a graduate level pastor and that is fine. But let's be careful about prescribing the same for all churches.

While planting my first church, we often held evangelistic Bible studies in the homes of church members. We would go door-to-door and invite neighbors. Usually some would come and at least one person would become a Christian or rededicate their life to Jesus.

Dede Mustill attended one such neighborhood Bible study. She rededicated her life to Christ and began attending our church. After a while her husband Ted also began to attend. Raised in a Catholic background, Ted was somewhat antagonistic and skeptical toward the Bible and Christ but eventually the Gospel took root and Ted became a believer. He quickly grew to have a vital relationship with Christ.

A few years later, the Mustills moved to central California and began attending a small local church. When the church lost its pastor, the congregation asked Ted to become the pastor. But Ted was reluctant. He and Dede visited our home and talked with Carolyn and me about it. They explained that the church was not evangelistic and they saw no hope of it ever reaching out to the lost. Instead, they were thinking about starting a church themselves. They asked what I thought and although Ted had no formal theological education, I said "Ted, if that is the leading you feel, then I think you ought to go for it."

That was about ten years ago. The church they started in that rural community now runs about 250 in attendance. While many churches in the United States want a pastor with many degrees, Ted has something more important; a deep passion for the Lord and His work. I am thankful for my formal education. But all around the world God is using people like Ted to plant many fine local churches.

ARE HOUSE CHURCHES A BETTER CHOICE?

There are some clear benefits of house churches. House churches don't need to worry about building a building. It doesn't take much money to cover expenses. It's pretty simple to branch out to add another house church. House churches that run into persecution are harder to destroy because they move from place to place, and so on.

Depending on your ministry context, house churches may work very well. In other situations and countries, house church ministry may not be as practical or desirable. Often people in First World countries expect a larger body with a full variety of ministries for children, youth and so on.

So what kind and size of church do you want to start? Your answer should be based on what you believe will most effectively reach your target area and take into account your spirituals gifts and calling. Is your vision a larger church with a building and a full range of ministries or smaller and more nimble house churches that might more quickly multiply into a strawberry patch? As long as they perform the biblical functions of a local church, then either is great. While in the first three centuries the church may have more closely resembled the house church movements of today, that model may not be the most effective in all contexts.

SOME IMPORTANT QUESTIONS AND ANSWERS

Often when teaching on daughter church planting people will ask variations of three basic questions. Let's consider these questions one at a time.

1. *"What's wrong with planting a church within our church—like a new college ministry or a senior's ministry?"* My answer is that any ministry which expands the Kingdom is commendable and such ministries are likely to expand the church. The principle is: new groups (classes, Bible study groups, video venues, Sunday School classes, branches, preaching points, etc.) usually mean *new* people and that usually means *more* people following Jesus.

However, we should be careful about calling such ministries a "church," since the biblical elements of church discussed earlier are probably not all present. For example, such groups may or may not practice the Ordinances (baptism and communion) and are normally not led by a plurality of elders. Structurally, they are part of a local church, but they are not in themselves a local church.

A bigger danger is to allow the development of new ministries within a church to distract us from planting more churches since that's the most effective and most biblical method of reaching our prime objective – to reach the world for Christ. Also, most new ministries tend to address local needs while we are supposed to move beyond our "Jerusalem" to our "Judea," "Samaria," and the ends of the world. Focusing only on our "Jerusalem" does not encompass the full extent of Jesus' mandate. The best scenario is not an either/or but a both/and approach.

2. *"Isn't starting a 'video venue' or a new 'preaching point' a form of church planting?"* For those unfamiliar with these terms, a "video venue" is a ministry method based on video technology. Instead of insisting that everyone attend service in one room, churches can set up several sites both

on and off the main church grounds. The music styles and the audiences can be quite different but everyone listens to the same sermon which gets relayed by video tape or live video feed. These video venues are designed to appeal to people with different needs or preferences than those who attend the main worship service.

Video venues work well to target subgroups like college students or street people within the same church structure while utilizing the same teaching. In a mega-church, smaller "venues" can provide a smaller church atmosphere while still enjoying the benefits of being part of a large church. They can also reach more people than could easily fit into one sanctuary.

In video venues the pastor's sermon is transmitted electronically to different locations. When the preacher travels and conducts the same worship service at various outlying areas, these are often called "preaching points" or "satellites." As with video venues, the "preaching point" is a part of the larger church and usually carries the same name, but might be distinguished through descriptions such as "west campus."

Are these ministries "church planting?" How do they stack up to our definition of church? If they are permanent extensions of the main church, they are not autonomous local church plants. A lot depends on the makeup of the particular group and the plans of the mother church. For instance, a video venue geared for high school students will never become an autonomous church plant. But, if the mother church lays the proper groundwork such as training up local leadership, preaching points may well turn into daughter churches.

There are good reasons to consider a both/and approach and continue the planting of churches while starting "video venues" or "preaching points." But if a church has limited resources, it is more strategic to plant churches. Video venues aren't as useful to reach people in other languages and preaching points are limited to the scope of the local mother church. (Another downside of venues is that many churches who are planting them seem to be using them to reach more Christians, rather than pre-Christians. Depending on the focus and DNA of the Mother Church, a video venue *could* be a new means of evangelism. BUT, it also could simply be another opportunity to invite church transfers to join the church.)

Church Multiplication seems unlikely to occur through a video venue or preaching point, but more likely to happen through a daughter church. Since the New Testament places such high value on the autonomous local church, and since planting new churches has been found to be the most biblical and most effective method of evangelism, churches should view daughter church planting as a necessity no matter what other wonderful ministries they have.

3. *"Our outreach strategy is to start more groups within our church—isn't that good enough?"* This is another form of the same question. Starting more groups is wonderful and I hope you start a ton of them. But don't stop short of fulfilling the fullness of the Great Commission and utilizing the most effective and most biblical strategy to do so. Our methodologies should answer the question; "what will most effectively fulfill the Great Commission?" This Commission is not for a region—it is world encompassing.

Some churches are good at reaching out to the world through missions programs, but are deficient in reaching their Jerusalem. Others are reaching their Judea, but not their Samaria. Still others are reaching their Jerusalem, but are not reaching out to the world. Is it time to add some balance to your outreach? Where are you weaker—maybe you can strengthen your impact through utilizing the most biblical and most effective means of outreach: church planting.

IN SUMMARY: Don't make daughter church planting an either/or question. A both/and approach is a necessity. Yes, multiply cells (small groups, Sunday School classes, home Bible studies, etc.) within your fellowship to reach your region. But don't forget to multiply local churches to utilize the most effective and most biblical method of reaching the world for Christ.

CHAPTER SUMMARY

In this chapter, we have seen some of the exciting things God is doing through Church Planting Movements. We have examined the definition of "church" and in doing so sharpened our goal in daughter church planting. While affirming cells, video venues, preaching points and other forms of "branch" ministries from a church, we have affirmed the necessity of continuing the planting of daughter churches.

Prayer Points: How you can pray about the concepts in this chapter:

- Pray that the Lord blesses your church with significant growth at the same time that you plant daughter churches.

- Pray for the multiplication of Church Planting Movements around the world.

- Pray for the health and purity of both the Universal Church and each Local Church around the world.

- Pray for a balanced fulfillment of the Great Commission.

Action Steps: What you can do to begin to implement the steps in this chapter.

- Study the points in this chapter.

- Clarify your conviction of the biblical definition of "church."

- Visit other ministries that are expanding through daughter church planting to learn and stretch your thinking.

- Consider how you might reach the four spheres of the Great Commission through your life and your church: your Jerusalem, Judea, Samaria and the uttermost parts of the earth.

---

1 Rick Warren, *The Purpose Driven Church: Growth Without Compromising Your Message & Mission* (Grand Rapids: Zondervan, 1995), p. 180-181.

2 David Garrison, *Church Planting Movements: How God is Redeeming a Lost World* (Midlothian, VA: WIGTake Resources, 2004), p. 21.

3 Garrison, p. 35.

4 Garrison, p. 49.

5 Garrison, p. 65.

6 Garrison, p. 99

7 Garrison, p. 260, 261

8 Garrison, p. 271

9 Garrison, p. 271.

10 Gene Getz, *The Measure of a Church* (Ventura, CA: Regal Books, 1975; ninth printing, 1980), pp. 15, 16.

11 Robert Saucy, *The Church in God's Program* (Chicago: Moody, 1972), p. 148.

12 Wayne Grudem, *Systematic Theology* (Grand Rapids: Zondervan, 1994), p. 913.

Chapter 5

Ordinary People, Ordinary Churches, Extraordinary Church Families

So how exactly does daughter church planting get rolling? Of course God can use megachurches with megaministries and megabucks. But the vast majority of the time God delights in using ordinary people in ordinary churches. In this chapter I'd like to tell you some of their stories, starting out with my own.

MY STORY: FINDING THE BEST GOAL

Planting a church turned out to be harder than I expected. Starting with just my beloved wife, a handful of mostly flaky people, a living room to meet in and very little money, my goal was just to **survive**. After years of incredibly hard work, deep pain and intense joys, our church finally reached about 225 in average attendance. I felt that we had finally attained viability. We survived!

What next? I breathed a sigh of relief, sat back and began to dream about growing a more successful ministry. **Success** became my goal and I measured success in attendance numbers, new programs, and building a major ministry that would put us "on the map" of our denomination. I studied and earned a doctoral degree in church growth.

I had some major lessons to learn. It surprised me to discover that many people in my church were not so concerned with growth. As long as things were going well, they did not want to rock the boat. They were more interested in maintaining the **status quo**. As hard as I worked to grow the church, some of them seemed to work hard to reverse my efforts and maintain the current situation.

Survival, success and status quo are inferior motivations for ministry. They are understandable, and in some ways laudable. That is why so many churches and church leaders are hypnotized by them. But God has designed us for a greater purpose.

My friend and mentor Dr. Bob Logan helped me grasp a greater motivation: **significance**. One day when I was feeling pleased with my achievements, Bob shook me up by looking me in the eye and saying, "Now that your church has reached viability and strength, you need to begin giving birth to daughter churches."

Internally, I bristled at the idea. What did he say? How could he suggest such a thing? It felt like Bob was recommending that I abandon my dream of a large successful church and instead "shrink" my church to plant others. After my years of blood, sweat and tears, that was about the last thing I wanted.

But you know the rest of the story. Giving away resources and people to plant New Song Church gave our church and my ministry far greater significance for the Kingdom of God than we would ever have achieved otherwise.

HAL SEED'S STORY: SETTING EVANGELISM GOALS

It thrilled me to see what happened after New Song Community Church, our first daughter church, launched in 1992. Let Pastor Hal tell it in his own words.

> We had led enough people to Christ before the launch and during the first year that I decided to write it down and keep a running total. By Sept. 27, 1993, our one year anniversary, there were 92 first time decisions.
>
> In 1995 there were 53 decisions (about one every week), which made me think, "What if we could be like the Acts 2 Church and lead a person to Christ every day?" So I prayed that God would let us lead one to Christ every six days in 1996, every 5 the year following, etc.) We led 63 to Christ in 1996, 79 to Christ in 1997.
>
> When I shared this "one a day" goal with our Strategic Planning Team, they said, "Going from one every two days to one every day is a doubling. Let's set ourselves a more realistic goal. So we added the intervening year of 1.5 days (243 goal). But we hit 513.

The grand total saved in 2005 went above 2,500. New Song has its own building now and has helped plant four other churches.

TULSA AND ALBUQUERQUE: TINY BUT MIGHTY

Many church leaders are tempted to say that because of their limited size, shortage of finances, lack of leaders or other reasons, they simply cannot plant a daughter church at this time. This is akin to the widow who gave her mite saying, "Since I have only a penny, I will give nothing. Maybe some day when I have more resources I will give." Thankfully, she gave what she had. Jesus blessed her gift with a greater commendation than those who had much and gave out of their surplus.

Therefore, God must be very pleased with churches like The First Church of God in Tulsa, OK, which had just 55 people in average attendance in 1985. Nevertheless, they had a big vision for the lost. Instead of saying, "We only have a mite, so we cannot be involved in daughter church planting" they said, "We only have a mite, but with the Lord we have His might." So they sent their pastor and 25 people, plus a few thousand dollars to plant a new church nearby. It was NOT A SPLIT; it was an intentional act to fulfill the Great Commission.[1]

The Eastside Wesleyan Church in Albuquerque, New Mexico is another example of a "Widow's Mite Church." Pastor Jim Turner led that church of 71 in average attendance to embrace a vision to plant another church on the west side of Albuquerque. So in 1998 they sent out 24 people and $5,000 to plant on the west side of town. God is surely pleased with their "West Side Story."[2]

PASTOR MOORE'S STORY: REACHING 10,000 IN HAWAII

In the early 1980's Pastor Ralph Moore moved to Hawaii, not far from Honolulu, to plant a church. He asked God to give him His vision for the new church. The Lord gave him the vision of reaching 10% of his area – roughly 10,000 people. Instead of trying to grow one big church, he envisioned planting 100 churches of 100 people within ten years.

They held their first church services on the beach! Eventually they found a place to meet and their church grew significantly. But they never gave up on the vision of 100 churches of 100 people in ten years time. They talked about their goal constantly.

They started new churches by developing leaders from within their own main congregation. If a leader could grow a small group to a significant size, and if God was calling him to church planting, they assisted him in launching his own congregation. Rather than formal theological education, they focused on the Biblical qualifications of pastoral leadership found in I Timothy 3 and Titus 1.

*MARK AND CAROLYN
WITH RALPH AND
RUBY MOORE, 2004*

So, did they reach the goal? Yes and no. Within eleven years they started 35 churches. Better yet, those churches were reaching over 10,000 people in total attendance. Given the 60-80% salvation statistic we saw earlier, they probably reached 6-8,000 lost people for Christ! By now, years later, Moore's church has planted over 200 daughter churches.

*RALPH MOORE'S
MOTHER CHURCH
LITERALLY MEETS IN
A TENT, BUT ON THE
SIDE HANGS THIS
LISTING OF SOME OF
THE 200+ CHURCHES
THEY HAVE PLANTED*

DAVID REYNOLD'S STORY:
PLANTING DAUGHTERS BEFORE BUILDINGS

Brand new churches can plant daughter churches in their early years; before they own a facility. David Reynolds planted ShoreLife Church in 1991 in Huntington Beach, California. ShoreLife helped plant five churches during its first seven years while meeting in a rented school building the entire time.

In 1998 David moved to Washington to found Northwest Church Planting out of New Heights Church. NWCP has helped hundreds of church planters throughout the northwest and beyond.

In May 2003, "bitten" by the church planting bug again, Dave moved to Southern California to launch Chorus Church envisioned to become another church planting center. Chorus started with just one family but two years after launch is now preparing to launch her first daughter, Creation Church, once again long before owning their own facility. The mother church is hoping about five families from the mother will form the nucleus of the new church and, of course, tithe to help support it. They are giving $500 per month, in addition to financial support from the denomination. They plan to send temporary volunteers to help since the daughter will be close by.

DR. P'S STORY: THE VISION FOR 1000 INDIAN CHURCHES

Church leaders in third world countries do not let the lack of money or even persecution stop them. Dr. Paramanandam (we call him Dr. P.) of Chennai, India has a vision to plant 1,000 churches all over India. Saved from a Hindu background in 1969, Dr. P. founded the Calvary Baptist Church in 1978. He is an accordion player and street preacher. The music attracts a crowd and then Dr. P preaches Jesus. In his church of about 200 people, most are converts from Hinduism, and others converted from Roman Catholicism or Islam.

India has 1,600 languages and Dr. P realized that he must train young men from around India who speak the languages. He founded a Bible college which offers a Bachelor of Theology degree. Tuition is free as Dr. P does his best to raise funds. Last time I checked, students were still sleeping on mats on the floor. On their extremely limited budget, they make the most of every rupee.

Graduates have thus far planted 105 churches (some are admittedly in early formative stages). A few have buildings and the rest meet under trees or in small thatched huts. Poor in terms of the world's resources they are rich in spirit!

DR. P

Hindus get upset when people convert to Christianity. They give Dr. P trouble in many ways. He writes, "They tried to kill me many times. I received two letters telling that they are going to kill me and drink my blood. I am not afraid of my death. One day anyhow we are going to die. Let me die for Jesus. If they kill me, I am going to be with the Lord in Heaven. If I am alive, then I am going to plant 1,000 churches all over India. I am sure that nobody can kill me before God's time."

FIRST BAPTIST'S STORY: MOTHERHOOD IN OLD AGE

First Baptist Church of Doylestown, Pennsylvania was founded in 1846. It has had a significant ministry, but had never been a mother church until it was 150 years old. Then, Pastor Dan Young spearheaded the daughtering of Cornerstone Community Church in Perkasie, PA. Led by Pastor Doug Knepp, in its first five years Cornerstone has grown to 125 people each Sunday and over 50 people have been baptized through its ministry.

The testimonies are inspiring. Pastor Doug brought back stories of people who had been delivered from drug addiction and alcoholism, marriages that had been restored, people who found joy in following Christ and sharing their faith with their circle of friends. Wonderful stories like this are common in new churches.

It's no wonder that although Pastor Dan had served the Mother Church for 15 years, he said that planting a daughter church was the most enjoyable thing he has done in his ministry at First Baptist. So he led in a second daughter plant in the year 2001. That plant is New Hope Community Church in New Hope, PA, a community known as a center for witchcraft and the homosexual community.

Pastor Chuck Wilson writes: "New Hope Community Church had quite a start in September of 2000. A group of homosexual activists tried to shut the church down before it got started. There were picketers and police on a regular basis for the first few months, which we considered free advertisement. We were attacked in the papers and on TV on a regular basis. God showed us how to fight hate with love. We began an AIDS Ministry, which prompted a leader in the gay community to comment that 'although we know you don't agree with everything we believe, we know that you care about us.'

"In two and a half years, New Hope Community Church is averaging 150 in Sunday attendance and has led 30 people to Christ with 26 baptisms. At a recent baptism in the Delaware River, we experienced a touch of heaven as the Holy Spirit poured out in a special way. People were openly weeping as they shared from the water's edge about God's deliverance from alcoholism, drug addiction and sexual bondage (homosexual and heterosexual). Their testimonies touched every heart as we realized afresh God's mercy and grace."

REV. BRYAN'S STORY: PLANTING DESPITE PERSECUTION

Rev. Andrew Bryan was born into slavery in 1737 and grew up a slave on a plantation in South Carolina. In 1782, Andrew and his wife were saved. A few years later, he planted a church consisting mainly of slaves, many of whom were soon forbidden to attend his services because their owners feared the message of freedom in Christ. Many who did attend were flogged and severely punished. Even Andrew was whipped, beaten, imprisoned and his church was seized. Andrew's master, who supported his ministry, helped arranged his release from jail.

Andrew purchased his freedom after his master died. In 1794, several influential whites helped him raise the money to purchase property on which to build a new church, the first black Baptist church in the US. Within six years, the church had grown to almost 700 members, truly a mega-church in that day. It was called the First African Baptist Church of Savannah. However, Andrew's goal was not simply to have a large congregation and impressive church so in 1802 he deliberately split the congregation and planted a new church: the *Second* African Baptist Church of Savannah. The church growth continued and in 1803 he again split the church, forming The *Third* African Baptist Church of Savannah. As these churches grew, their congregations pioneered churches in other parts of the state. The ministry of Andrew Bryan and his daughter church planting brought thousands in Georgia to a personal relationship with God through Christ.[3]

Rev. Andrew Bryan *The first black Baptist Church in the US*

AN AFRICAN VISION:
PLANTING CHURCHES AROUND THE WORLD

Christ Apostolic Church of God Mission Inc. began in a humble elementary school in Benin City, Nigeria in 1974. The founder, Rt Reverend Apostle Dr. S.E. Ogbonmwan, is a man raised for this generation and for the world. Although he is blind, he has a vision for evangelism through church planting. Through his vision and the mighty work of God, the mission has planted 96 churches in Nigeria and twenty other churches around the world in places like Canada, Belgium, England, and the USA. This is amazing given the limited resources in their homeland.

The goal of the mission is soul winning – their motto is, "Evangelism, our supreme task." They accomplish this mission by training nationals to go to all parts of the world. The founder's son, Dr. Matthew Ogbonmwan, now leads the continued efforts to reach the world for Christ. In 2005, when I spoke for their bi-annual gathering in Houston, Texas, I marveled at their commitment to the task. Their founder does not speak English and their resources are still very limited, yet their impact is worldwide.

THE EAST 91st STREET STORY: PLANTING MEGA CHURCHES

In 1985 the E 91st Street Church in Indianapolis, Indiana envisioned starting twenty daughter churches in twenty years. They finished within seventeen years. Many of their daughter churches have also become megachurches. Their new goals are as follows, taken from their website.

We believe that God is calling East 91st to be a leader in a dynamic new era of church multiplication. We sense His leading for a new faith-stretching dream – a dream so big and bold we can only accomplish it by the power of God. The New Testament church witnessed a great harvest of souls as, "the Lord added to their number daily those who were being saved" (Acts 2:47).

We want to experience that same multiplication of believers and churches throughout the unchurched regions of the United States and Canada. We believe our goals reflect the heart of God for reaching lost people in the twenty-first century. Specifically, our goals entail the following:

1. E91 will plant 65 daughter churches by 2010.

2. The daughter churches will reproduce themselves. The goal here is to move from addition to church multiplication.

3. We will recruit 25 megachurches to partner in church planting by 2010 and these churches will plant an additional 50 churches by 2010.

4. We will establish five Strategic Church Planting Centers by 2010.

5. At least five of our daughter churches will be from among different ethnic minorities residing in North America.

This mother church keeps a close maternal eye on their church plants. Every year they have a church planting weekend. They invite all the daughter churches to come. The congregation stands and applauds them. They call them their church's "heroes." They maintain a bulletin board that displays the name, location and start date for their daughter churches. They look for ways to stay in touch and to celebrate new church starts. They continually remind the congregation that this is what "you" are doing to build ownership of these goals.

Rev. Jim Penhollow, the Minister of Church Multiplication at East 91st Street Church, states, "Large churches are stewards of greater resources and therefore have greater responsibility. We must have an Acts 1:8 outlook: Jerusalem, Judea, Samaria and the uttermost ends of earth. It is like concentric circles. We have to have balanced vision of reaching people everywhere and if we do not have a strategy, we won't do it. Church planting is the strategy for Judea, Samaria and the ends of earth. It is a no-brainer, it is our responsibility."

Pastor Penhollow shares how it all funnels down to the fact that real live people become followers of Christ because of church planting. He recalled the testimony of a couple who accepted Christ in one of their daughter churches. The couple shared how they are now moving to another area to witness to people in that neighborhood. Another man was an atheist but became believer through a church plant. He shared Christ with his family, three coworkers, and a Mormon friend and all have been saved. Jim says, "Stuff like this is the bottom line, not just reshuffling the deck between churches."

JOIN THE EXCITEMENT!

Picture the faces of people coming to Christ:
- A biker, with a scraggly long beard, leather jacket, earring.
- A teenage boy, complexion pimpled, headphones playing music, skateboard
- A mid-twenties mother, new to parenting and wanting to give a spiritual legacy to her children
- A retired school teacher, looking at the final years of life and needing hope for eternity
- A four year old girl, innocent about life with a heart wide open to the Savior

Those are the faces of people being saved through new churches such as the ones above. They are the faces of folks in communities all over the world who are open to the Truth if someone will reach out to them with the Good News of Jesus. Will we reach them? Will we do what the Apostles did when Jesus thrust them into the world as He gave His Commission?

CHAPTER SUMMARY

In this chapter, we have seen the stories of churches large and small, wealthy and poor, from around the world, which are reaching lost people through daughter church planting. Through these efforts, thousands of new believers now follow the Lord Jesus Christ. God is looking for other churches to join them in this valiant mission. Why not your church? Why not you?

What story does God have for you and your church to tell?

Prayer Points: How you can pray about the concepts in this chapter:

- Pray that churches around the world capture the vision of evangelism through daughter church planting.
- Pray for pastors to prioritize the harvest.
- Pray that daughter churches also reproduce to produce a movement of evangelism and church planting.

Action Steps: What you can do to begin to implement the steps in this chapter.

- Study the points in this chapter.
- Ask friends to introduce you to reproducing churches.
- Visit churches that have multiplied. Interview the leadership.
- Go on a prayer retreat and pray for a vision of the network of daughter churches your ministry might reproduce.

Chapter 6

Answers to Objections to Parenting

Chances are that since you are reading this book, you have overcome many of the excuses against daughtering a new church – at least to your own satisfaction. But you also have to convince others influential leaders and help them to resolve their questions, objections, hesitations and doubts.

This book has already examined many concerns. In this chapter I will provide help in answering twelve specific objections you may encounter. You might need to adapt these arguments to fit your unique circumstances. If you run into others, check out the longer list of objections in the *Dynamic Daughter Church Planting Handbook*. It is a step-by-step guide to planting a daughter church for both the mother and daughter churches. Available from Dynamic Church Planting International, www.dcpi.org.

Objection #1: We'll lose our church fellowship.

Stacy, who attends church in St. Cloud, Minnesota, put it this way. "When I heard about starting the new church in Avon I was very apprehensive because a lot of the people that were going were close friends of mine and we had been worshiping together here for many years. As the time came to send them I got caught up in the excitement and the joy to send them and wish them well."

The members of Christina Fellowship Church of Liberia also experienced these same misgivings, according to Rev. Wellington Morris. "Many people were unwilling to leave their comfort zones. Some were afraid to launch out in a strange area to plant a daughter church. What we did … was to pray and sensitize the church about the urgency of beginning a daughter. And we ourselves took the initiative of going out to begin a daughter church, as the pastor, which encouraged the members to join in the campaign."

Core team members are actually missionaries to a new community, even if they don't cross a sea to get to their mission field. Besides, the average person only knows a few people really well. The rest are casual acquaintances. It would be tragically shortsighted to deny people the opportunity to hear the Gospel through a new church because we want to see some casual acquaintances once or twice a week.

Some core groups may face more daunting hardships. Dr. Paramanandam shares what happened when one of his church planters preached the gospel in a new village in India. The high caste villagers opposed him, objecting to his efforts. "I suggested that he stop going to that village and start praying to God. When he returned to the same village and preached the gospel they were very receptive. Within two months, we will be planting a church in that village."

Objection #2: It will cost too much.

"We do not have the material, financial and human resources to begin to start another church....Who will be the pastor? Who will pay their church planter if we get them to come from another place?" Pastor Richard Vah, a West African pastor faced the concern voiced by many churches the world over. Careful and creative consideration, however, may reveal just how affordable a daughter church can be!

Daughtering a church may not involve any cash outlay at all, depending on how the daughter church is structured. Often the funding can come from a variety of potential sources:

- a denomination/association
- support raising done by the planting pastor
- from the core group
- through a pastor who is bi-vocational

In large mother churches, the regular giving by a sizeable core group may contribute a significant income to the new church. For example, when Community Baptist Church of Alta Loma, California planted a church, it allowed its former youth pastor, Dennis Larkin, to recruit a core group from within the church and also to raise support from members who remained in the mother congregation. That raised enough support and the church itself didn't need to budget funds.

Smaller churches can use the same strategies on a smaller scale. Look for outside sources of funding. This helps to build a larger team for the project. As more people contribute funds, they will also be inclined to pray, to volunteer their help and to find needed office equipment and supplies.

The fact is that with creativity and God's provision, **any** church can become a mother church. Beyond any monetary gifts, churches can provide people, oversight, denominational covering, and the use of their facilities. Furthermore, funds given will be a wise investment. Peter Wagner writes "There is no more practical or cost effective way of bringing unbelievers to Christ in a given geographical area than planting new churches."[4] So give all you can and help others do the same!

Objection #3: We're too small.

Many churches and pastors feel that their church is not large enough to be a mother church. Since the church is struggling just to survive, to make its budget and to reach its own community, "giving birth" seems impossible.

When is a church too small to help in daughtering a church? The answer requires answering another question: what level of involvement in the project do you hope to achieve? If the only option is to completely conceive of the project, recruit the founding pastor, fully fund it, send a significant core team, buy property for its first building, and so on, then only a handful of churches in the world are "big enough" to daughter a church!

On the other hand, churches of any size can have a significant impact on planting a daughter church if they are part of a team that contributes to the project. Pastor Kevin Marsico puts it this way. "Size is not the issue; attitude is. Leadership must help the congregation to think BIG, dream BIG and act BIG. Otherwise, small size translates into small hearts and even smaller impact. We teach people that size is not a limitation; for God, it's an opportunity, an opportunity for Him to show what He alone can do, to get all the credit for the results and to draw more people to Himself. For us at Community Baptist Church in Weymouth, Massachusetts, we lived by Hudson Taylor's credo: 'Expect great things from God; attempt great things for God.' And we planted five new congregations in six years, even though we never broke 150 in attendance."

In summary, it's not the size of the church that counts; it's the size of the vision that matters. If you have the vision, God can do great things through you.

Objection #4: We can't afford to lose the leadership and workers.

Who will join the core team of the daughter church? Our experience is that those who volunteer may possess one or more of the following characteristics:

- an entrepreneurial, pioneering spirit
- a heart for reaching lost people
- a missionary zeal and giftedness
- a level of dissatisfaction with the mother church
- an attraction to the vision and/or pastor of the new daughter church

Although some current leaders or active lay people decide to join the core group, often the new project will attract people who were completely uninvolved in ministry in the mother church – spectators who perhaps don't feel they are really needed there. However the chances are very good that they will become leaders and workers in the daughter church due to the pressing need for help in a startup congregation. Dan and Debbie Proctor, whom I mentioned in Chapter 3, are good examples. In the mother church they were spectators. In the new church they became key players.

When leaders and workers do leave a mother church, often new leaders and workers emerge from within the mother church to shoulder the tasks the departing core group members left vacant. Mother church leaders might have to pray for workers and work hard to recruit them.

Sometimes the folks who join the core group would have left the mother church anyway. Commissioning them to start a daughter congregation sends them off with joy and purpose; as opposed to watching them simply drift away.

One church had a vocal group of members who drove from an outlying area and wanted to start a daughter church in their hometown. The church leadership discouraged the idea because they wanted to build a bigger building instead. They undertook an aggressive fund raising plan.

They built the building but the families left anyway and started the church. Others left as well and the original church became a shadow of its former glory. What a shame that they didn't embrace the vision to start a daughter church. They could have taken godly credit for a project that ultimately succeeded. Instead, they missed God's pleasure and the blessing of daughtering.

Objection #5: It will destroy our growth momentum.

Too often pastors and churches care more about the growth of their own corner of the kingdom, rather than the growth of the whole kingdom. It's true that daughtering a church may affect growth momentum in the mother church: it might decrease or it might increase. But the more important question is: How will daughtering affect the growth of Jesus' Kingdom? The answer is clear: Christ's Kingdom will grow. So we should work to build His Kingdom and trust God for what happens in our own corner of the Kingdom.

The right attitude is not, "My kingdom come, my will be done" but, "Thy kingdom come, Thy will be done."

Working through your church's level of involvement will help you determine how much to invest in the daughter church. Through focused prayer you will sense what the Lord wants you to do to best enhance the opportunity for the daughter church to do well, while at the same time maintaining the viability of your own congregation.

Keep in mind that God may choose to replace your investments almost immediately. Or He may see fit to allow you to wait for His blessing. But He will always reward those who invest in His Kingdom. "Command them to do good, to be rich in good deeds and to be generous and willing to share. In this way they will lay up treasure for themselves as a firm foundation for the coming age, so that they may take hold of the life that is truly life" (1 Timothy 6:18-19).

Lutheran Pastor Ken Ferber can testify to this. "When we began twelve families chose to go to the new church. I was thinking we are already having a problem with our budget. This is going to be difficult to lose these families. We, however, knew that this was the Lord's will so we committed them to the Lord and had a special sending service. Three months later we had a new member Sunday at our church. Two and one half times the number of people we sent to the new congregation joined that day. God gave us almost seventy new members!"

In other parts of the world this can be a more complex issue. Pastor David Badio of Royal Family Church describes how they handle the special challenges faced by African pastors. "The philosophy of the African community is one where family is extended and lives in one community and one big family as communion people. They have lived by inclusion strategy where when their child passes 20 or 25 years of age they stay in the same home or compound. Independence and individualism is hard. This is why marriage is arranged and approved by the family which actually is a community. For an individual or a small group to decide by personal conviction is hard in some cases. These have been the objections. The way out now is that we have decided to use the family model of every home a worship cell group. So our people are seeing that as our home groups get more and stronger – we are increasing in attendance and so more people are ready to do other new works."

Objection #6: Our church won't go for it.

John Gonleh, pastor of the Union Baptist Church in Liberia, expressed it this way. "To spread the gospel in order to reach the unreached is outside the approach of former church planters and pastor/missionaries. So it is not in the DNA. People resist change, and would not establish a fellowship to meet both spiritual and physical needs of the people because they thought this would affect the existing community ministry resources. We overcame this resistance by prayers, great timing and constant meetings, repeating the vision in many forms. This encouraged the people to see mandates and its urgency."

You may face an uphill battle to "sell" the idea of daughtering a church. But spiritual leadership means helping people to understand what's important to Christ and then helping them to do it. If people aren't familiar with the idea of being a mother church they might have some initial reluctance. People need help to do the right thing. That's what godly leadership is all about!

We've already discussed some suggestions for sharing the vision but let's review a few.

Preach about it so that your people understand the Biblical model of spreading the Gospel through church planting. Teach topically on evangelism and church planting. Use testimonies and get personally involved so you can share your enthusiasm. Send your people to see first-hand what God is doing through other mother and daughter churches.

Work to win key opinion leaders first. Let's face it, unless the key people in your church buy in, it will probably never happen. Be careful of getting ahead of these key leaders. Work with them one on one as necessary to bring them on board.

Pastor Isaac Ross of the Church Planting Mission of Africa reports that they struggled to begin daughter church planting because it hadn't been done before. "There was no knowledgeable person to mentor, coach and lead the team and so there was fear of failure…. We as leaders took the lead to begin focusing on house church by family home devotions and Bible studies (as cell or satellite groups). This helps…the whole church to see the picture."

Regardless of your situation, give the process of persuasion some time. Some leaders will tend to move too fast. Find the rate at which your congregation can accept this new paradigm. And allow your church to begin at lower levels of commitment. Depending on their level of ability, allow your church to increase their level of tangible and intangible commitment with each new daughter church.

Objection #7: The leadership just isn't available.

Some may want to daughter a church, but believe that they can't find the pastoral leadership to make it happen. While it may be impossible on a human level, with God, all things are possible! When we pray, He has promised to provide: "The harvest is plentiful but the workers are few. Ask the Lord of the harvest, therefore, to send out workers into his harvest field" (Matthew 9:37b-38). I'll talk about this in more detail in Chapter Eight. For other helpful instructions on recruiting church planters see section three of *The Dynamic Daughter Church Planting Handbook*.

Objection #8: But pastors get kudos for bigger churches, not daughter churches.

This may be one of the biggest barriers to daughter church planting. Yet you will probably never hear it spoken out loud. It's a little too personal, honest and selfish to speak about publicly. Yet I know from personal experience the temptation in a pastor's heart to build his own flock and ignore the fact that he could reach more people through also planting daughter churches. Pastors of big churches gain career recognition and self-esteem.

How can pastors overcome this temptation?

Some simply need to learn more about it. Since they really do want to serve Christ well, I believe most pastors would be receptive to the idea of daughtering, once they discovered how effective it is. They need encouragement to redefine success to mean kingdom impact more than congregation size.

Sometimes a pastor may need to get away with God to give Him a chance to grab hold of their heart. The decision to daughter is a big one. A time away with God and His Word may provide the spiritual fortitude necessary to take that next mountain!

Pastors can benefit greatly from practical support and affirmation, both from associations that trumpet the efforts of mother church pastors, and from encouraging key leaders within the church. Don't let daughtering be a thankless job. It's the old principle, "What gets rewarded gets done." Most pastors have a busy schedule. Daughtering a new church is just one more project that sounds great, but they can't do everything. So, chip in to help by shouldering as much of the load as possible.

Objection #9: Since so many existing churches are struggling, shouldn't we concentrate on revitalizing them?

People watching their church decline often verbalize this objection. They mourn the decline and want help to revitalize their church before they start new ones.

However, it is virtually impossible to reverse the trends of a declining church. As someone said, "It is easier to have babies than to raise the dead!" Should we abandon declining churches and just let them wither away? Absolutely not. But we should recognize that it's a better use of energy and resources to begin new congregations.

Established churches tend to turn inward. They usually do not have the evangelistic fervor that new congregations do. Does this have to be the case? No, but with notable exceptions, most churches follow this pattern. Growth comes primarily through new life.

Let's not answer this question as an "either/or," but as a "both/and." Older churches should try to reach the lost the best they can. But at the same time, we should plant new churches recognizing that they will be on the evangelistic cutting edge.

More churches reach more people. Even churches within the same denomination develop different philosophies of ministry, different church personalities, different styles of preaching and music and emphasize their own doctrinal fine points. Lost people benefit when they have more options.

Objection #10: We tried it before and it didn't work.

It's discouraging to watch a baby church die. When I was five years old, my mother gave birth to a premature child that my parents named Scott. My brother Scott lived only about ten days. It was a difficult period for our family. But if a child dies, does that mean you never try to have a child again? How sad that would be. My parents did not give up; they had two more children, Jonathan and Claudia.

What if everyone who failed the first time quit? How many babies walk the first time they try and never fall? How many children ride a bike the first time they try and never crash? How many baseball players never strike out?

Look at the Scriptures; did Paul succeed everywhere he went to start a church? No, in fact sometimes he was stoned, beaten, left for dead.

God does not ask us to bat a thousand in church planting. He asks us to be faithful. The question is "Will you quit, or will you go on?"

One church planter planted four churches and then failed in his fifth attempt. He felt like quitting and nearly did. Nevertheless, he tried again and that church was a tremendous success. It was the largest church in town from day one. Over four hundred people came to Christ in seven years. What a tragedy it would have been if he had quit because of one failure!

Objection #11: This is a bad time for us to daughter a church.

Some may object that they just don't have the time to invest in a new church plant. That is understandable…but not excusable. There may be times that are more conducive to planting than others. On the other hand, times may never get better. In the meantime, people are dying and going to hell. If we are looking for excuses, any time is a bad time. Please be careful about postponing daughter church planting for a better time.

You may say, "We'll plant when we get to, say, 500 in attendance." But what if you never get to 500? Most churches don't. In fact, most don't even make it to 200. Saying you'll wait until you grow to a certain size is probably saying you will never do it.

For some, there may be an element of selfishness to this objection. It's almost like saying, "I'll build my kingdom first, and then I'll build Christ's Kingdom." But how can that attitude please Christ?

The time to reach out and utilize the most effective evangelistic strategy is now!

Objection #12: I don't know how.

Some people would like to plant a daughter church, but they don't have any idea of how to do it. The next section of this book will give you some starting steps. For more thorough instructions, get a copy of *The Dynamic Daughter Church Planting Handbook*. You may also want to attend a training seminar sponsored by DCPI where our vision is "to impact the planting of one million churches to reach the world for Christ." To order resources or find out more about training events, visit our website at www.dcpi.org.

CHAPTER SUMMARY

In this chapter, we looked at answers to some common objections to daughter church planting. Open hearts can overcome these objections. I hope this chapter will encourage a great discussion in your church.

Prayer Points: How you can pray about the concepts in this chapter:
- Pray that your church can discuss and overcome objections in a spirit of love and peace.
- Pray that other churches will do the same.
- Pray for a wave of daughter church planting in your area.

Action Steps: How you can begin to implement the steps in this chapter.
- Ask your leaders to work through this chapter with you and discuss the answers to objections that are most likely to occur in your congregation.
- If you are a teacher in your church, integrate answers to these objections into your teaching.
- Examine your own heart in light of these objections. What is holding you back? What is the Lord saying to you about your own objections?

---

[1] From a conversation with Jim Moss, East Pennsylvania Churches of God, General Conference, 1999.
[2] From a conversation with Phil Stevenson, 2000.
[3] *The WallBuilder Report*, African-American History Issue, 2005.
[4] C. Peter Wagner, *Church Planting for a Greater Harvest* (Ventura, CA: Regal Books, 1990), p. 21.

PART TWO

THE *STTARR* PROCESS:
A PRACTICAL MODEL
FOR GIVING BIRTH
TO HEALTHY
DAUGHTER CHURCHES

So, now that I hope I've convinced you to daughter a church, the next big question is "How?" It can seem like a pretty daunting goal – sort of like trying to reach the stars. The good news is that many churches have done it successfully. In Part Two we will break this project down into bite-sized pieces and show a workable plan to get it done. Not only can we reach the stars, we can be stars. There's a great verse in Daniel that I love.

─────────── CHURCH REPRODUCTION THEME VERSE ───────────

"Those who are wise will shine like the brightness of the heavens,
and those who lead many to righteousness, like the stars for ever and ever."
─────────────── (Daniel 12:3) ───────────────

As a teen, I dreamed about becoming a famous Christian music star. Some people dream of being a sports star, movie star or other kind of celebrity. In middle age, I realized that being a celebrity is not a very worthy goal, and it probably wouldn't have made me as happy as I imagined.

But this verse reveals what *is* important – to be a star in God's sight, not just for fifteen minutes of fame. This Scripture tells us how we can be God's stars who "shine like the brightness of the heavens for ever and ever." That is truly a goal and purpose worth living for! How does it say we can achieve that lofty goal? Answer: "Lead many to righteousness." That means leading them to salvation. The way to be a real star is to bring people to Christ. Our goal ought to be to take as many people with us to heaven as we can when we die.

Now, that's a star! I will never be a Billy Graham or Apostle Paul. Compared to stars like these, I am a flickering candle. But I still want to do all I can to reach the world for Jesus. Maybe you feel the same way. If so, may I suggest that the way we can shine the brightest is to be a *STTARR* in planting daughter churches.

As I've thought about the process most successful people go through to plant a daughter church I came up with an acrostic to help keep the stages in order using the letters STTARR. We will explain each step more fully in the following chapters. Here is what the letters stand for in the *STTARR Process* for daughter church planting.

THE *STTARR PROCESS*

S = <u>Share</u> the Dream of a daughter – get your church on board

T = <u>Think</u> About Your Involvement – determine your level of participation

T = <u>Team</u> Leadership – find the church planting pastor and other staff

A = <u>Attract</u> the Core – mentor, provide internship and recruit the Core Team

R = <u>Rejoice</u> – give birth and celebrate

R = <u>Reproduce</u> – nurture the daughter and reproduce more new churches

Before we get started, let me make a few comments. Part Two is intended to introduce you to this process, not get you bogged down in detailed training about each step. We will fly over the landscape so to speak just to give you a flavor of the issues you will need to handle in each stage and to help you to see that, with God's help, you can do this.

When you get to the point of actually implementing these steps, we have many practical resources available for you at DCPI and elsewhere. At the end of each chapter I will include a resource guide. All of these steps are explained in more depth in *The Dynamic Daughter Church Planting Handbook* available from DCPI (www.dcpi.org).

Also, I have written this book mainly for pastors and key lay leaders who are considering daughter church planting. So, if you are a denominational leader, this book will be most useful to you as a resource to challenge and encourage your people.

I realize that you have specialized needs as you implement a church planting strategy for your denomination. While this section will not address your unique perspective, please contact DCPI for more information on the many resources we offer to denominational leaders, especially in the areas of mentoring church planters and mother church pastors and creating a healthy climate for church planting within your district.

Chapter 7

Successful Conception: *ST*TARR

*ST*TARR = <u>Sh</u>are the Dream of a Daughter – get your church on board

The best time to begin envisioning, planning and sharing the dream of daughtering new churches is from the very first days in the life of a new church. So, **start sharing the dream from day one.** Continually communicate that a healthy church is supposed to reproduce itself. Don't just plant churches; plant reproducing churches.

However, if your church has no church planting vision and needs to be inspired with the concept of birthing new churches, there's still hope, but you may have to work a little harder to share the dream. Whatever your situation, consider these suggestions.

Begin with prayer and commit every step of the way to the Lord in prayer. First, we recommend that you get away for a day or two and spend time in prayer before the Lord. Giving birth to a daughter church is not a trivial matter. It takes specific focused prayer to get God's vision for daughtering new churches through you. Then, as you become convinced that the vision of a daughter church is from God, recruit others to pray with you. At first you might limit the circle of prayer partners but then broaden the prayer base as appropriate. Prayer will open the doors to the vision of daughter church planting.

Work to win key opinion leaders. Who are these people? They are the *formal or informal* leaders in the church that people look to for direction. They may or may not hold any official position on the leadership board or in another key role. Nevertheless, these are the people who are the de facto leaders in your church, the ones that others look to when opinions are being formed.

Without the approval of these people, your daughter project will be incredibly difficult, if not impossible. With their approval, others will generally come along. You will have a unified church, and churches will get planted.

Here are some strategies to help these key people become your allies.

Quietly identify five to ten key opinion leaders for every one hundred adults in your church. Look both for those who get things done, and those who stop or slow down progress. **Develop a relationship** with these people. Genuinely communicate love and care for them, their families and their concerns. If you care about them, they will care about you and your concerns. **Get to know their ministry felt needs and "hot buttons."** If you know their passion, you will be better able to speak their "language" and relate to their concerns.

Share the daughter vision with them one on one. You'll be better able to answer their questions, concerns and objections to daughtering before they voice them to their friends in the church. **Relate daughter church planting to their ministry hot buttons whenever possible**. For instance, if they have a passion for children's ministry, let them know that a new church will reach children for Christ. Then, **give them time** to process your new and perhaps intimidating ideas about daughtering a new church. Some will catch on more quickly than others.

Allow them to take the lead to persuade others. Once they are on board with the idea, give them opportunities to speak out on the issue. If they are shy about public speaking, then get their permission to quote their opinion. Let people know that the key opinion leaders are in favor of the idea of daughtering. (By the way, be careful not to publicly label them as "key opinion leaders." That can cause unnecessary misunderstanding. If they have a job title you can refer to that position. If not, just quote them by name.)

Now that the key leaders are on board, turn your attention to persuading the full church. Whenever possible, try to **answer people's objections before they are even raised**. Don't assume resistance, but calmly address the objections you anticipate people might have. This book has given you lots of suggestions in that regard. Keep praying for God to soften their hearts.

You can also use the power **of the pulpit to share the biblical mandate and benefits of planting a daughter church.** Preach on the need for outreach, church planting and daughter planting. You can incorporate that message into any number of sermon formats. After all, it is a major theme of the New Testament! Also, use other teaching forums such as adult Sunday School classes or small group series to educate your people. You might consider teaching people about the *STTARR Process*.

Regardless of the biblical texts and series you use to teach about daughtering, be sure to **highlight the joys of being a parent or grandparent**. People need guidance to capture a vision of the joy of parenting churches. Bring in other leaders who have successfully daughtered a church or two and give them opportunities to share the joys of being a "mom." Be realistic about the work involved, but frame the discussion as a positive long-term blessing.

Help your people to capture a bigger vision of what the church can do. Talk about planting a *family of churches*, churches that might even outlive the mother church. **Remind people that missions begin at home** and extends around the world. Far too many believers focus on the mission fields far away and forget about the mission field in their own back yard. Help them to see how daughtering a local church can help them to fulfill their part of the mandate in Acts 1:8 to preach the gospel in their own spheres of influence: their own Jerusalem, Judea, Samaria, and uttermost parts.

Many people learn best by seeing things firsthand. **Expose them to successful models of daughter church planting.** It can be extremely valuable to take people to visit both mother churches that are actively daughtering, and new churches that are being planted. Let them rub shoulders with people who are getting the job done. Let them hear in person the testimonies of people saved through the work of a new church. Let them get a vision for the joys of being a parent church.

Use creativity to inspire your congregation with the dream. For instance, you can create banners and video presentations, host conferences that highlight daughtering, start task forces, use bulletin inserts and newsletter updates, and host informational sessions and prayer meetings. Send your people for training and on tours of successful church plants. Get the children and youth involved. Send out volunteers of all ages to help with a nearby church plant just to get their feet wet.

What if your efforts to share the dream of being a mother church meet resistance? What if you get blank stares, objections or even outright "absolutely not!"? Should you conclude it must not be God's will and just give up? That might be tempting. But God wants the lost to be found and churches to be started. He wants us to do the right thing, even when it meets resistance.

So, **keep sharing the dream until others believe in it**. Always be kind and patient with people. Don't make enemies. Listen patiently and reason gently. Give people space to work through this "new" concept. Some may have been Christians for decades and never been involved in planting a daughter church. Work with the key opinion leaders. If they give you good suggestions along the way, take their advice. Keep addressing objections in a loving way. Most of all, keep praying. This is a spiritual battle because every successful daughter church plant represents new territory won for Christ.

When most of your people are on board with the dream of daughtering, congratulations – you have taken the first step! Now you are ready for step two.

STTARR: <u>Think</u> about Your Involvement -- Determine Your Level of Involvement

At some point, you will sense that the official leadership, the unofficial "key opinion leaders," and the congregation as a whole, are sufficiently in agreement with the idea of planting a new church. Well done, you're on your way! At this point the biggest issue is; "To what extent is your church willing and able to invest in a new daughter church?" There is no right answer regarding how much each church should be involved.

Now it is time for some serious decision making. Designate a team of people who will spearhead the planning and implementation of this project. You may choose to work through your existing official leadership board (however that is designated in your particular denomination or church). Or you may assign a team to make these decisions under the authority of your leadership. This team will need to make decisions in three broad areas:

- Developing a church planting philosophy and plan;
- Deciding whether to become a mother church or a partner church; and
- Determining specific involvement for the current church plant.

We will use the remainder of this chapter to explore these three major topics in more detail.

***

It is good to **develop a complete church planting philosophy and plan**. But churches will vary in their level of readiness to envision the future. If you feel your church is ready for an extended vision, we highly recommend that you develop a set of guidelines that will direct the planting of not just one daughter church but many.

On the other hand, you may need to share the dream of one daughter or partner church, work hard to make that project succeed, and then dream bigger the next time around. Either way, a complete philosophy and plan should address these topics:

- Biblical and practical reasons for planting daughter churches.
- The vision and goals for daughter planting in your church.
- The leadership and authority system you will use for the daughters.

- Procedures for target community selection, founding pastor selection, and drawing up the new church board.
- Philosophies regarding financial provisions, accountability, and independence.

View your commitments as minimal commitments. You may want to increase your help as the project goes on. Leave some flexibility to increase your commitments!

***

The second major issue to decide is **whether to be a *Mother Church* or a *Partner Church*.** What's the difference? A *mother church* shoulders the primary responsibility for launching the daughter church. Just as a human mother gives sacrificially to her child, a *mother church* gives sacrificially to bring new life. Typically, a *mother church* provides a crucial combination of these major kinds of resources: project oversight, church planter support, project support, core group leaders and workers, a prayer team, help with site selection, a meeting place, training, promotion, and possibly assistance with land and building.

On the other hand, a *partner church* comes alongside and helps a church planter and a new church with significant specific tasks but they do not shoulder the primary responsibility. A single new church plant can have one mother church and several partner churches. Or an established church can find a church plant that is already underway and choose to partner with it without taking on the major responsibility of becoming a mother church.

Whether your church chooses to become the mother church or a partner church, it is equally important to answer two questions:

"What are we going to do for the church planter and the new church?" AND

"What are we *not* going to do for the church planter and the new church?"

A church of 80 can have a crucial role in planting a daughter church. So can a church of 1500. But the capabilities of a small church may be very different from those of the larger church. Again, each situation is unique and the only "right" answer is to do what you sense God calling you to do. Whatever the answers, it helps enormously to clarify the issues for everyone involved. This avoids misunderstanding or uncertainty, both for the church planter and for the mother or partner church. If those questions are left unresolved it can cause strained relationships between the new church and the mother or partner church.

Whether you are a mother or a partner church, there are some intangible and non-monetary ways that you can help the church plant. These may include such things as providing core team members, a mentor or office space, sending prayer teams or teams to do demographic surveys, providing interim meeting places for the core group, donating equipment, and becoming an advocate for the church plant within the denomination and to other local churches.

Some churches may feel they are ready to be a mother church without any outside help. Even if that is true, there is a real kingdom benefit in involving other congregations as partners. So, **get help from your denomination and sister churches**. It gives the opportunity for others to become infected with the daughter church planting bug! And while the involvement of partner churches may be somewhat minimal at first, it may grow in time. So spread the joy around!

Many associations of churches have funds earmarked for church planting. They also have connections with potential church planters or other resources. These are part of the benefits of being involved in a fellowship of churches. Thank God for them, and take advantage of whatever your association is willing to contribute to the project.

If you have sufficient interest from one or more churches, you may want to bring representatives from the churches together for a vision and planning meeting. It feels good to be involved in a cooperative effort and know you don't have to go it alone. Allow them to be involved in the planning as much as possible. This will enhance the feeling of ownership by all the parties involved. If all goes well, excitement will build as you dream and plan together.

Thank God for all your partners from other congregations, but be careful to reserve participation on the New Church Board for experienced, mature leaders, preferably those with church planting experience. Not everyone who will participate in the *work* of the project is ready to be involved in the *leadership* of the project.

Each of the churches involved must determine their level of involvement. Encourage others to invest all they can! Don't be territorial. It is almost impossible to have too many resources!

Once you have done your best to get the assistance of your fellowship of churches, you will have a clearer idea about where the project stands financially. If the committed amount is large, praise God! If it seems low, don't lose heart. Allow God to provide in other ways. At least you know where things stand and what has to be done.

As I (Mark) wrote the preceding paragraph, two birds landed outside my window, just inches away from my desk. I watched them chirp and hop from limb to limb. They reminded me of Jesus words, "Look at the birds of the air; they do not sow or reap or store away in barns, and yet your heavenly Father feeds them. Are you not much more valuable than they?" (Matthew 6:26). God will provide!

***

By now, you will be able to **determine specific involvement for the current church plant**. These questions fall into three broad categories: budget, site selection and issues of control/ autonomy. We will discuss these in broad strokes as if you have decided to become the mother church, retaining authority to make all of these decisions. If you have chosen to become a partner church, some of these will not apply as much. But it helps to see them as part of the big picture.

Preliminary Budget. How much is this daughter going to cost? That is the first question some people ask. But it shouldn't be. The first question should be, "Is this what God wants us to attempt for Him?" If we are truly doing God's work, He will supply. Where God leads, He feeds. "And my God will meet all your needs according to His glorious riches in Christ Jesus" (Philippians 4:19). Dream big and watch the Lord provide. Big dreams attract big people and big money.

When you set this budget, you do not have to have all the cash on hand. Assess how much has already been committed, and what else needs to be raised. Below are some typical budget categories with notes about some of the items that might (or might not) be included as part of each one. You may, of course, have different items in your list, depending on your situation. Make realistic estimates in each of these areas. Raise all the money you can. Spend as much as possible on outreach to win the lost.

STAFF: Salaries, housing allowance, benefits, expenses, continuing education.

CELEBRATION SERVICE: Banners, stage materials, video projection unit, sound equipment, offering plates, communion cups, directional signs.

CHILDREN'S MINISTRY: Portable cribs, playpens, tables, chairs, curriculum, supplies, TV/VCR.

OUTREACH: Direct mail costs, logo design, outside signs, brochure, newspaper and telephone book advertisements.

FACILITIES: Church service facility rental, custodial services, office rental, utilities, liability insurance, storage containers.

DISCIPLESHIP: Bibles, materials, information table.

ADMINISTRATION: Secretarial compensation, office supplies, telephone, copier, computer needs, software.

CHURCH REPRODUCTION: Missions and church planting giving.

Site selection. It would probably be best to have a proposed target community selected before the church planting pastor comes on the scene. Or you may have several communities in mind. Sometimes the target community will be determined largely by the area where the core group lives. These decisions can be made by the committee or pastor in charge of the project.

Whoever decides should do so on the basis of several key factors. Learn as much as you can about the target area. What's the demographic makeup – what kind of people live there? Which areas are growing the fastest? Which areas are most unreached? What's the vitality of local churches? Does the area seem spiritually receptive? You may want to wait until the planting pastor can give significant input to this vital decision before making the final choice about the target community.

How close should the daughter church be to the mother and partner churches? You can plant a daughter anywhere – five minutes away or on the other side of the world. But, realistically, you will be able to make the most direct contribution if the daughter church is within a thirty-minute drive. That's because the most practical help a mother or partner church can give is to provide core team members. Participation will be easier both for short-term helpers and for long-term workers if they live nearby. If the church plant is fifteen to thirty minutes away from the mother, core team members will probably not feel the pressure to move to the new locality.

Now, if God is leading you to a location further away, He will also help you to find resources to complete the project. Keep these issues in mind as you consider the location. Ultimately, you will need to depend on the Lord to guide you for this important decision.

Level of control/autonomy and return on investment. Having determined what you will be giving to the new church, you also need to determine what you will expect from the new church. These expectations might be in the areas of:

- Financial return for future church planting;
- New church participation in mother and partner church functions;
- Participation in the next daughter church you plant;
- Accountability to your Board.

These kinds of expectations need to be spelled out ahead of time. Clearly written expectations at the beginning of the project go a long way toward preventing hard feelings or misunderstandings later. These expectations should be explained to the prospective church planting pastor as part of his call.

As you can see in this second step of the *STTARR Process*, we strongly recommend that you hammer out some clearly articulated agreements between all the parties involved in planting a daughter church. This prevents so many problems down the line. Choose your commitments wisely. It is best to under-promise and over-deliver.

One of our DCPI leaders might be able to consult with Mother or Partner churches to help you through the process of planting a new church. We can do this several ways, by consulting on-site, by working with your representatives who come to our headquarters, or by communicating via phone or e-mail. We strongly encourage you to attend DCPI's Churches Planting Churches (Daughter Church Planting) Conference in order to produce the most effective daughter church plant possible and to help you avoid strategic mistakes that can hamper and even destroy your efforts.

We have created sample worksheets and agreements that you can use to work through this process in an organized way. You can find them in the handbook mentioned below. Each step in the process of using them should be bathed in prayer by all concerned.

ADDITIONAL RESOURCES FROM DCPI (www.dcpi.org)
Book
The Dynamic Daughter Church Planting Handbook, by Paul Becker & Mark Williams
This is a complete how-to book for both a mother church and the daughter.
Profiles
Mother or Partner Church Commitment Profile, by Paul Becker
New Church Site Selection Profile, by Dr. Jim Carpenter

Chapter 8

Finding Leadership to Birth
a Healthy Daughter Church: *STTARR*

STTARR: <u>Team</u> Leadership – Find the Church Planting Pastor and other Staff

Here at DCPI, we have personally planted a number of churches and have worked with church planters all over the USA and in other countries. Based on that broad experience, we have concluded that the best model for planting a successful daughter church is to send **a leadership team of at least two fully-subsidized planters.** Now we realize that model may not be possible in every situation. But, it helps to state the ideal, even when it is impractical in particular situations. Let's unpack that statement briefly.

Both from a practical standpoint and from observing the New Testament example, we see that **church plants need leadership**. A few people in a living room may want to start a church, but unless someone with leadership abilities takes the group in hand, there's no telling whether that group will become a functioning church.

The Antioch church started without a leader. Ordinary Christians preached about Jesus and many people turned to Christ. But when the mother church in Jerusalem heard what was happening in Antioch, they wisely sent Barnabas to lead the new church. He quickly fetched Saul to help him (Acts 11:19 – 26). By chapter 13, the Antioch church had become well established with a good team of leaders.

Speaking of which, the New Testament is filled with examples of **team leadership**. Jesus sent out disciples two by two. Every missionary journey in the Book of Acts mentions a team of men who planted churches. They typically specified one person who led the team, but teams planted churches. This model has huge benefits: accountability, balance of gifts and strengths, mutual encouragement, multiplied efforts, prayer support, companionship, etc. It also provides the best practical experience to train the next generation of church planters.

Also, in most successful church plants, the sending agency **fully subsidizes the salaries of the church planters**, at least for a while. This also follows the Biblical model. Although Paul had been trained as a tentmaker and sometimes subsidized his income that way, usually he and his companions worked "full-time" in church planting, relying on the financial gifts of those who supported his ministry.

In fact, the Lord moved Paul to write a biblical mandate: "The Lord has commanded that those who preach the gospel should receive their living from the gospel" (1 Cor. 9:14b). Paul was not shy about asking for financial assistance either. He sought and received missionary support from churches he started. We believe it is best that church planting pastors be full-time in the ministry. It is appropriate for them to raise support by asking for assistance, just as Paul did.

If you are able to start with a fully subsidized multiple staff team, praise God. We believe this approach best fits the Biblical model. However, if you must start with only one staff member, or use a "tent maker" model, praise God for that too. Successful churches have been started under less than ideal circumstances.

***

So, **where do you find good church planters?** Again, ideally God will raise up a senior planter and support staff from within your fellowship. They have a proven track record. However, that scenario is rare, and many mother churches must search for qualified church planters.

Most churches are familiar with the regular search process for finding and selecting pastoral staff. So we will not discuss those procedures here. (The *DCPI Dynamic Daughter Church Planting Handbook* has a detailed discussion of this process.) For our purposes, I'll touch on three unique elements of searching for a church planter.

First, when you set up a **financial package** for the church planter, bear in mind that a generous salary package will pay you great kingdom dividends. "For the Scripture says, 'Do not muzzle the ox while it is treading out the grain,' and 'The worker deserves his wages'" (1 Tim. 5:18). You're only asking for trouble if you put a planter and family on a salary that makes it difficult for them to survive. Underpaid church planters will usually be less effective because they are distracted by pressing financial needs. The fairly compensated church planter can focus on ministry. Churches that skimp on benefits such as health insurance, vacation time, and sick leave, wonder why church planters burn out.

Secondly, a unique feature of the salary package for many church planters is some kind of **descending scale**. Often there will be several sources for funding: denominational resources, commitments from the mother and partner churches, financial support raised by the church planter, and – gradually – income that begins to come from the new church. Typically, the salary package is structured over a period of several years in a way that shifts the responsibility for providing the salary to reflect the growing capability of the new church to contribute.

Thirdly, let's focus on the **unique characteristics** to look for when searching for a church planter. Church planters are a specialized breed because church planting is a unique undertaking within the larger arena of pastoral ministry. Over the years we have seen unhappy results when mother churches or denominations choose a planter without taking this into account. For instance, the following people may, but more likely, may not be well qualified to plant a church:

- Good-hearted amateurs who seem to have a burden for reaching people.
- Pastors who can't get a job in an established church.
- Mavericks who want to "do their own thing" and be on their own.
- Future overseas missionaries who want planting experience before going overseas.
- Anyone crazy enough to try it!

So what does make for a good church planter? We will answer that question in several ways. **First, learn to think like a church planter**. Watch for these characteristics:

- Church planter types **like to develop something out of nothing**. They are trailblazers. They enjoy things that are fresh and new.
- They tend to **think outside the box**. Their theology is probably orthodox, but in other

ways they have a nontraditional outlook. They look for creative ways to reach lost people.

- They're **resource gatherers**. Starting a church with no building, few leaders, no programs, and little money is slightly scary for them, but it also adds to the allure. They enjoy discovering the pieces needed to put the puzzle together.
- They **respond to a big challenge**. Telling a church planter that something can't be done is actually highly motivational to them. They tend to live by the motto, "The difficult we do immediately; the impossible just takes a little longer."
- They are **risk takers** who are not afraid to fail.
- They have a **pragmatic approach to getting the job done**. Like Paul, they have a "whatever it takes" attitude toward the task of reaching lost people and growing the church (1 Cor. 9:19-27).
- They have a **heart for lost people**. Church planters typically see the harvest and are highly motivated toward reaching lost people.
- They are often **not particularly denominationally minded**. They are bored by bureaucracy. In fact, because of their non-institutional thinking, they may be turned off by denominational politics and traditions. They may consider denominational involvement a distraction from their main job of reaching lost people and starting churches. (This can irritate denominational leaders who would be wise to establish an agreement regarding denominational involvement up front.)
- They **appreciate straightforward communication and clear commitments**. Many church planters are "straight shooters." They say what they mean. They appreciate the same thing in return. They don't feel they have the time to pussyfoot around important issues.
- They are **independent minded and like being their own boss**. Church planters dislike supervisors who hover and micromanage them. It is important to give church planters lots of freedom and minimal control. Nevertheless, they still need mentoring and accountability.

Of course, not all church planters have all these traits. But these are typical of church planter types. We are not saying that you, in the mother church, have to like these characteristics or be attracted to them. In fact, some may irritate you. But these traits define a church planter and help him succeed. Being aware of them will help you recognize a candidate you wouldn't necessarily select for a staff position in the mother church but who would make a fine church planter.

Now, that's a big list of qualifications. Do they have some overarching themes? Yes. One of the best church planting recruiters we know is Jay Nickless, the Associate in Church Planting with the Churches of God, General Conference, based in Findlay, Ohio. Jay looks for two crucial abilities as he talks with potential lead church planters: **Evangelist and Entrepreneur**.

He must be an **evangelist** since the goal of church planting is to build a new church by reaching lost people for Christ. If the planter is not gifted evangelistically, either the plant will die because it doesn't grow or it will grow by attracting mainly Christians. Neither of these is desirable.

He must be an **entrepreneur** since he is building a completely new organization. If he is not entrepreneurial, he may lead people to Christ, but not know how to set up the practical structures and programs to provide a solid place for growth. For awhile people who attend the church plant may find it exciting to be part of a baby church, but eventually, that loses its charm if the planter can't organize the plant into a functioning church.

Before we move on, there is a third paradigm by which to evaluate potential church planters. It isn't enough for a candidate to have the basic temperament to be a church planter. Our close friend Dr. Jim Carpenter observes that effective church planting leadership flows out of the confluence of three personal dimensions: **maturity, personality, and ability**. The effective church planter must have a depth of godly maturity that will sustain through the difficult process of planting a church. Also, the planter should have mastered the basic skills and received adequate training to accomplish the mission. You can read a fuller discussion of this evaluation tool in our profile called *How to Improve Your Church Planting Leadership*.

Whenever possible, **meet with the planter and spouse together**. This will affirm the spouse and help keep both key decision-makers informed. This also gives you the opportunity to express compassionate concern for the church planting family. You should evaluate the spouse as well as the potential planter. The spouse doesn't need to possess the qualities we've mentioned, but rather be compatible with the planter, and enthusiastic about the church planting project.

Church planting is a wonderful ministry, but it's not the only one. Some people who want to plant churches aren't really equipped to do so. Therefore, you need a careful **assessment process** for potential church planters or team members to determine whether they are called and qualified. Your denomination may provide assessment. Many couples have found our *Pre-Assessment Profile* helpful as they consider church planting.

I have one last comment about **additional church planting staff**. Again, it isn't necessary that every team member be a classic church planter. Your goal is to field a team that covers all the bases needed to accomplish the mission and that works well together. If you can send out a team, we suggest that at least one team member have good administrative skills because this tends to be a weakness for many of the best church planters.

Finding the right church planter is a tremendous milestone. Once completed, thank God— you're on your way!

STTARR: <u>Attract</u> the Core – Mentor, provide Internship and Recruit the Core Team

Once you've chosen a planter, it is time to help him begin the exciting hands-on work of church planting. This extremely important phase happens before the new church's first public worship service and helps your planter lay a solid foundation.

MENTORING

In their excellent book on mentoring, *As Iron Sharpens Iron*, Howard and William Hendricks list five benefits of mentoring.

A mentor:
   ❖ Promotes genuine growth and change.
   ❖ Provides a model to follow.
   ❖ Helps you to reach your goals more efficiently.
   ❖ Plays a key role in God's pattern for your growth.
   ❖ Influences to benefit others in your life.[1]

Church planters *really* need mentors! Church planting is incredibly difficult, often lonely and downright overwhelming. It takes place on the front lines of spiritual warfare, and can destroy those without an adequate support network. Too much is invested in a church planting project to leave the plant and the planter vulnerable, potentially *demolished*, through neglect.

Bob Logan mentored me in my first church plant. His thriving church plant was a few years older than mine. I thought of calling him to get some pointers. But he called me and offered his assistance. Over the next few years he mentored me in many different aspects of church planting. We talked by phone frequently, met together face to face, and attended training conferences together. Bob started a small training workshop for church planters which I attended. He gave me assignments and held me accountable to complete those tasks.

Bob had a tremendous impact on my formation as a church planter. Frankly, without Bob's mentoring, I'm not sure my church plant would have survived. If it had died in infancy, kingdom resources would have been lost on a failed plant, our small core would have been extremely disappointed and I would have been deeply wounded, perhaps even dropping out of ministry.

Because mentoring is so powerful, we believe that providing a mentor is a vital component in the process of church planting. Ideally the mother church will select and assign a mentor. Of course, the planter can have input in the selection, but the onus should be on the mother church to appoint one. If the mentor asks for an honorarium, we suggest that the mother or partner churches pay for it.

What makes for a good mentor? This list of responsibilities and qualifications for the daughter church planting mentor can guide you in your selection:

Responsibilities:
1. Hold mentoring appointments at least biweekly during the start up phase and at least monthly after launch. Each meeting should last one to two hours.
2. Care for both the planter and the new church.
3. Hold the planter accountable to perform steps necessary to develop the church.
4. Attend a pre-birth worship service to evaluate and encourage.
5. Participate in the New Church Board.

Primary qualifications:
- A heart for the daughter church plant and a passion to see it succeed by reaching lost people for Christ.
- Some church planting experience.
- A genuine concern for the church planter and his family.
- A good listener.
- The ability to give guidance in a loving manner.

The mentor should immediately help the planter to prepare a **timeline** for the launch of the new church. Check our handbook for detailed instructions on preparing this timeline. This invaluable tool helps the planter keep track of the dozens of details involved in planting a new church. After scheduling the timeline, you may want to adjust the details and dates depending on how much progress you make and other factors.

The mentor holds the planter accountable to do the timeline tasks. Some planters are very schedule oriented and need little motivating. Others need lots of guidance and prompting.

INTERNSHIP

A healthy core group is the best resource a mother church can provide for a daughter. These committed people provide both the initial manpower and a beginning financial base for the new church. They provide the backbone of the new congregation.

How can a mother church provide such a core group? People can't be forced to join the core group. They need enough information and inspiration to feel called by God to voluntarily join the new work. They must believe in the dream and in the church planting pastor.

The best way to raise a core group is to give the planter some time in the mother church so he can get to know people, and they can get to know him. We call this time an "internship" with the mother church.

A Daughter Church Planting Internship gives the church planting pastor time to do two things:

1. To recruit core team members from the mother church and partner churches.
2. To lay the foundation for the new church launch.

We recommend an internship of six to twelve months before launch. A shorter time will probably not give enough opportunity to recruit and lay the foundation for a great launch. A longer time might be helpful for foundation laying but also might be de-motivational to core team members, supporters, and others waiting for the church to begin. Be flexible. You may need to adjust the launch date based on how the internship is going.

We recommend that during this internship the planter be given a **temporary job title** such as Pastor of Church Planting or Daughter Church Planting Associate, making it clear that he is there mainly to launch the new church. The internship might also give him additional ministry experience. But you don't want to give the impression that he is a permanent addition to the church.

We also recommend that you send your daughter church pastor to a **church planter training seminar**, ideally also sending the spouse and the mentor. DCPI holds its Church Planter Training several times throughout the year. Schedule this as early as possible in the process of daughtering. In our training we have planters map out their VPT – vision, plan and timeline for the new church. This foundational work needs to be done sooner rather than later.

This internship can sometimes become an awkward period. Do human mothers and daughters ever have a hard time getting along? You bet they do! Likewise, mother and daughter churches sometimes experience poor communication, misunderstandings, and hard feelings. While this is not inevitable, it is *possible*. So be ready to help facilitate healthy communication, and to work through difficulties should they arise.

The senior pastor of the mother church can help facilitate this internship by doing several strategic things.

- He can keep setting the vision before the whole church.
- He can give the planter VIP exposure through preaching opportunities and other high-visibility meetings.
- He can actively participate in recruitment setting up appointments with potential core team members.

- As pastor, he can shepherd his people through their personal decision-making process.
- He can help screen potential core group members.

As the specific needs of the new daughter church become better known, many mother churches host a "**baby shower**" for the new church. The mother church can publicize the specific wish list to the many organizations, partner churches, well wishers and others who are committed to the success of the daughter church. In addition, area businesses might be willing to donate items.

RECRUITING

You may find your core group members in the mother church, among new converts, from out of town recruits, staff members and spouses, etc. When you set a goal for core group size, you'll want to set a goal that is both visionary and realistic, given the realities of your ministry setting. Bigger churches can potentially send larger core teams. More church planter staff members will attract and hold more core members.

Optimum core team size in most cases will range from twenty to sixty adults. Large mother churches often set larger goals. But we should warn you, larger core teams can actually become counterproductive because they tend to focus on their needs and ignore lost people in the target community. A large and powerful core team can be the tail that wags the dog. This is usually unconscious – the core probably won't realize they are limiting outreach by focusing of themselves and forcing the staff to do the same.

Give people plenty of opportunities to learn more about vision for the new church. Tell them about your goal of reaching the lost, the people you will "target," where the church will locate, how it will start, what style of ministry it will have, and so on. The church planter needs to enthusiastically share his dream for the new church. The mother church pastor, daughter church staff team members and core team members can all participate in casting this vision.

We recommend that people who are considering this decision be carefully screened to make sure they will be an asset in the new church. Church planting appeals to lay people for a variety of noble and not so noble reasons. The mother church pastor should meet personally with all potential core team members to discuss their motivations for joining the new church. These meetings will help to form a relational bond with the core team members. He will want to help them work through any negative motivations. This may involve repairing broken relationships with people in the mother church. It might mean encouraging manipulative people not to join the new church.

Core team members need to fully agree with the type of ministry envisioned, including the style of music, the hoped for size, the number of services, the cell group philosophy, the average age of the target community and so on. Those who don't may prove to be a hindrance rather than an asset.

Encourage people who pass this recruiting hurdle to make a formal commitment to become core team members for the new church plant. You might have them sign a written covenant.

Some people who won't be ready to make such a firm commitment might be willing to provide short-term volunteer help. Welcome them. A new church needs all the help it can get! Don't look a gift horse (or volunteer) in the mouth! Some may even find they prefer the new church and will join up later.

One warning: Don't give *leadership* positions to people who won't make a firm commitment. This can send wrong signals to the core team that even the top leadership isn't really committed to it. Also, if those leaders drop out, it can seriously affect morale in the core team. Certainly people will come and go in any church. But try to prevent this from happening with top leaders in your church.

As soon as possible, the planter should begin holding **regular core team meetings** to prepare for the launch of the new church. This format has been helpful to many:

- ***V. Vision.*** Include worship, prayer, Scripture, and testimonies of what God is doing.
- ***H. Huddle***. Allow individual ministry teams time to work together and plan for the launch.
- ***S. Skills.*** Train how to share your faith, how to greet newcomers in the church, how to have a quiet time, how to start a new ministry in the church, etc.

Use these meetings to keep **people informed and to celebrate "wins"** together such as people coming to Christ, spiritual growth of core members, new groups started, funds raised, equipment secured and so on. Develop an environment of excitement and enthusiasm.

Meanwhile, the church planter will recruit another special group of pastors and others with experience in church planting to help advise him. These will form a temporary **New Church Board**. As newcomers to the church prove their qualification for ministry, these outsiders to the church will gradually roll off this board until the new church can set up its own Elder Board.

CHECK OUT THESE RESOURCES FROM DCPI

DCPI Pre-Assessment Profile, by Dr. Jim Carpenter

How to Improve Your Church Planting Leadership: A Three Dimensional Approach, by Dr. Jim Carpenter

The Mentor Profile: What it Takes to be a Mentor and Why Church Planters Need Them, by Dr. Jim Carpenter

How to Develop a Leadership Board for Your New Church, By Dr. Mark Williams and Paul Becker

---

[1] Howard & William Hendricks, *As Iron Sharpens Iron* (Chicago: Moody Press, 1995), p. 25-31.

Chapter 9

Birthday Celebrations and Family Expansion: *STTARR*

STTARR: <u>Rejoice</u> – give birth and celebrate

Most of the work leading up to the launch of the first public services for the daughter church must be done by the church planters and the core group. They will work hard finding a place to meet, reaching out to people in the community and advertising the launch date. They will aim to be ready by launch date to handle the needs of the people they hope will attend the new church. They will work hard to provide such things as Sunday School, nursery, small groups, discipleship, and evangelistic outreach. Especially as the date draws nearer for that "Birth Day," the mother church will step back to let the team do its work, because she will have already provided those most basic resources which we mentioned in the last chapter.

But the launch date of public services provides another crucial time for the Mother Church to provide invaluable assistance to maximize the impact of their daughter's birth day. This is a once in a lifetime opportunity to help their daughter have a good strong start. In this section we will suggest ways that the Mother Church can help the daughter church have a great Launch Sunday.

Do All You Can to Make the Launch a Major Event. If you capitalize on this launch date, it can actually generate more momentum. At DCPI we teach church planters ways to gather many people for the first Sunday. Often the Birth Sunday has the biggest attendance for the first few months. Building on that strategy, use the Launch Day as a springboard for further outreach and growth. Try out these ideas:

• *Contact local media for coverage.* Radio stations, TV stations, and newspapers are looking for newsworthy events. The birth of your new church is one of them, especially when mother and partner churches collaborate to launch a new congregation. Sometimes churches receive front-page coverage of their launch.

• *The mother and partner church pastors should attend the launch service if possible.* This will both inspire them and encourage the daughter pastor and team. Be careful that everyone understands the main focus that day is on outreach and the lost. Core team members and well-wishers from the mother church should agree beforehand to delay their fellowship until all the guests have gone. Furthermore, visitors from the mother church should help out if needed to pray, pick up chairs, greet people, clean up, and so on.

• *Include special prayer for the daughter's launch in the mother and partner churches.* Try to arrange for a prayer team to cover the whole Launch Sunday in prayer. Use email, denominational newsletters, and other methods to ask others to pray.

• *Record the day.* Find a good photographer whose only job that day is to record the event in pictures. If this means paying a few dollars to hire someone to photograph the event, it will be worth it. The daughter will have only one birth. If you can videotape the event, do that as well.

• *Coordinate your promotion efforts with those of the daughter pastor and team.* The left hand must know what the right hand is doing for this important day.

Promote the Birth in the Mother, Partner and Other Churches. Share the joy with all the churches that helped make the Launch Day possible. Give praise to God, encourage those who sacrificed for the plant and inspire others to plant daughter churches to reach the lost. The daughter church won't have time to do this. The church planter will already be overwhelmed. But nobody will mind if the beaming Mother Church pulls out her pictures of the new baby. Start right away.

Use eyewitness testimonies. Beginning with the mother church pastor, give those who attended the launch opportunities to share their excitement. Show the video in the mother church. Make a collage of the photos and put it on exhibit. Invite new converts to come to the mother church to give their testimonies. Nothing tops the testimony of a new Christian to reward those who have sacrificed so much to bring a new church into being.

Get the word out within your denomination. Send them write-ups and photos to include in denominational newsletters. Sharing these glory stories can encourage other churches to plant daughters of their own.

Overcome "Postplanting" Blues. Over 80% of women who give birth experience some degree of "postpartum blues."[1] This happens even to women overjoyed about having a new baby. Usually this condition stems from fluctuations in hormones, insecurities about one's ability to be a good mother, financial fears, exhaustion, isolation, family problems and the like. Likewise, mother churches and their pastors may experience "postplanting blues" – a season of depression or anticlimax in the weeks or months after the launch of the new church. This can be confusing, especially if your daughter church is healthy. You may wonder how you could possibly be depressed when God is blessing.

But this is perfectly understandable: you may have sent out some of your best workers; your finances may dip because the core group redirects their giving to the new church; you may be exhausted from the effort of giving birth; you may experience the predictable letdown that often happens when you accomplish a major goal.

How can you overcome postplanting blues? These suggestions have helped us:

- *Take time to get away with God and pray.* Thank Him for the privilege of giving birth and rejoice in the new people reached for Christ through the new church. Ask the Lord to renew your spirit and your vision.
- *Rest.* Elijah became depressed after the confrontation on Mt. Carmel depleted his energy. Just like him you need to rest to recover your equilibrium.
- *Concentrate on the positive.* Steer your attention to the good things happening both in your ministry and that of the new daughter church. "Fix your thoughts on what is true and honorable and right. Think about things that are pure and lovely and admirable. Think about things that are excellent and worthy of praise" (Philippians 4:8b New Living Translation).
- *Believe that God will reward your faithfulness.* "Remember this: Whoever sows sparingly will also reap sparingly, and whoever sows generously will also reap generously" (2 Corinthians 9:6).

Make Your Congregation Aware of the Numbers. They might also feel letdown if they notice the attendance numbers dip. It can encourage everyone to report the *combined* attendance of the mother church plus daughter(s). While the mother church attendance may initially drop after sending out core team members, when you add together the attendances at all the churches, the total will likely climb higher than the attendance the mother church experienced before daughtering. And don't forget to keep track of decisions for Christ.

We don't value numbers for their own sake. That's wrong. But God was so interested in numbers He included a book in the Bible named "Numbers!" Several times in the Book of Acts Luke recorded how many people converted to Christianity. Churches carefully count the offering. Are offerings more important than people? We count people because people count.

In Luke 19 Jesus told the parable of the talents. He emphasized that our Master wants us to invest wisely whatever He entrusts to us. We too can see returns of fivefold or tenfold or even more! One day the Master will return to see what we did with what He entrusted to us. He will reward us based on how we have multiplied our resources as a mother church. *He will be counting – shouldn't we?*

Keep Good Records of Vital Statistics. When a baby is born, many people ask about the vital information: the birth day, birth weight, length, and, of course, the name. Likewise, be sure to keep careful records about your baby church. Obviously, the daughter church will gather this statistical information. But they will be busy. You need to make sure that it gets done.

In addition to the raw attendance numbers, ask the planter to track such things as professions of faith, re-dedications, baptisms, memberships, and small group attendance. This will be most useful in the long run if it includes names, dates, and other pertinent details. This can be done on a Monthly Church Planting Report, which you'll find in the *DCPI Daughter Church Planting Handbook.*

Encourage People to Visit the Baby Church. Most family members want to go see a new baby! It may be a pudgy, hairless, burping infant, but relatives want to see it and celebrate! When they do, their hearts warm toward the newborn child. Similarly, many people from the mother and partner churches will be eager to visit the new baby church. Encourage them to go. Nothing inspires more than seeing a new life. It will uplift them and the baby church as well.

However, encourage sensitivity about the timing of these visits. That first day can be overwhelming. The church planter and core team members are trying to greet as many unchurched guests as possible. It may be best to wait a few weeks until the dust has settled a bit. Even then be careful not to distract the team from reaching out to their emerging flock.

The pastors, staff and boards of the mother and partner churches should especially arrange times to visit the new church as their schedules permit. They will come away energized and enthused by what God has done through them. Their enthusiasm will encourage their own congregations.

STARR: Reproduce – nurture the daughter and reproduce more new churches

Ask any new mother and she'll tell you that the work really begins after she gives birth. It's the same for the new church. Pulling off a big birth celebration is easy compared to the tough job of turning that "crowd" into a "congregation." Sadly, some churches start with a big splash that proves to be just a "flash in the pan." Ultimately we want the big start to result in a long-term, healthy, vibrant, mature, God-honoring, and reproducing "adult" congregation.

So who bears responsibility for the long term health and growth of the daughter congregation? The mother church? The New Church Board? The church planting pastor? The core team? The best answer is "yes" to all of the above. Some bear more responsibility than others, but all should work together to make sure the church is a long term success. And keep in mind that "Unless the Lord builds the house, its builders labor in vain" (Psalm 127:1a). Unless everybody relies on God's power and guidance, no amount of effort will make it a success.

In this section we'll discuss ways that you as a mother church can help your daughter church to thrive.

Encourage the Church Planter and Core Team. Church planting is extremely hard work. Enormous effort goes into starting a church from scratch, work that is often lonely and unappreciated. People can become discouraged. Workers may drift or quit. The new church can flounder. It is not unusual for team members to suffer from exhaustion and burnout. Here are some ideas to prevent fatigue and burnout.

• *Provide opportunities to rest*. Don't set up situations guaranteed to burnout the core group. For example, rotate your children's workers so they get regular chances to attend "big people's" church services. Don't strand them for months on end without any break. This idea of rotating teams also applies for other ministries like set up crews and sound crew. You can periodically send borrowed workers to provide much needed rest.

• *Express appreciation*. People will serve more enthusiastically if they feel their labor is noticed and appreciated. Say thanks in person, write notes, arrange for appropriate gifts and awards, and remind them of your ongoing prayers.

• *Provide opportunities for workers to grow*. Being a core group member should result in spiritual growth, not decline. So make sure the new church offers an array of growth experiences through one-to-one discipling, small groups, core team meetings, seminars and workshops, retreats, and conferences.

• *Listen to needs and concerns, both personal and ministry related*. Just knowing someone is listening means so much. Acting on concerns and making changes or meeting needs encourages people even more.

• *Hold regular Leadership Team Meetings for all leaders, both staff and volunteer*. Use these meetings to hold one another accountable, to share praises and prayers, and to coordinate calendars. Take time to evaluate ministries, share vision, and give updates. Getting together reminds leaders they are part of a team. It enhances their ownership of the ministry and keeps them encouraged.

Determine if Additional Assistance is Appropriate. After the launch, the level of continuing involvement by the mother and partner churches should depend somewhat on the strength and health of the daughter. Even though you will have already determined your level of involvement, now is a good time to assess the actual vitality of the daughter church. Does the new church need more help in a specific area? Do they have enough musicians or children's workers? Would it help them most if you loaned some temporary help or if you helped them to recruit or train in some other ways?

Most new churches lack elder quality leadership. Even if they have some quality potential leaders, the Scripture warns not to "be hasty in the laying on of hands" (1 Timothy 5:22). Continued involvement in the New Church Board will be extremely helpful. An immature board can kill a baby church. How long this help will be needed depends on how quickly elder quality leaders emerge in the new church.

Ongoing mentoring for the church planter is a must. Even if he is an experienced planter, he needs this encouragement, care, accountability and guidance. Now might be a good opportunity to assess whether the existing mentor is working out well and to make appropriate changes if needed.

ANSWERS TO COMMON QUESTIONS ABOUT FURTHER ASSISTANCE:

Should mother and partner churches feel obligated to help a daughter church that seems to be struggling? You can feel good about sticking with the initial agreement you made regarding your level of involvement – you don't have to help more. However, if the daughter church clearly needs more help, feel free to do more as you feel led. Think and pray and then put in writing what else you will do. Remember the guideline to under-promise and over-deliver.

Is it possible to help "too much?" Sometimes new churches seem like great big bundles of needs. As in raising children, you should find a balance between helping too much and helping too little. Be as generous as possible to give your daughter a strong start. But guard against enabling an ongoing dependency relationship. Everyone will be better off if you encourage your daughter church to become self-sustaining.

We have seen instances where mother churches assist unhealthy daughters for years, long after it is clear that the daughter will never become viable. This is not a good use of Kingdom resources and it usually hurts the daughter church in the long run.

Yes, it is hard to end support for a struggling church. This is why it is so important to determine involvement levels for mother and partner churches beforehand. Do as you feel led.

What if the new church doesn't survive? The church, the body of Christ, is a living organism. Just as some babies die, so do some baby churches. It's unrealistic to expect every baby church to survive. Some denominational groups lose as many as 70% of their new churches![2] We think that's too high. Especially among the church planters we train, we see a new church mortality rate closer to 25-33% and that seems more reasonable.

Church planting is not a guaranteed endeavor. Even the Apostle Paul didn't always succeed. In fact, some cities ran him out of town! In Antioch of Pisidia, he gave up trying to plant a Jewish church, and instead planted a church among the more responsive Gentiles. He didn't quit. He didn't say, "If I can't succeed every time then I'm not going to try at all." Instead, he licked his wounds and kept right on spreading the Gospel through church planting.

Naturally, we want every church to survive and thrive! We should do all we can to produce a healthy vibrant congregation. But if a church doesn't make it, then we should learn from our mistakes, resubmit ourselves to God and keep on keeping on.

Continue to Nurture a Great Mother/Daughter Relationship. Although you made commitments to a great relationship, you should remain vigilant. If the relationship becomes strained it can thwart further expansion of the Kingdom via church planting. Mother and partner churches may hesitate to plant another church if they feel they got burned before.

So, you need to work at it. We suggest again that the mother church take the initiative in this because the daughter will be distracted with the wild ride of getting the church going.

Invite the daughter pastor and other daughter church leaders to present updates to the mother and partner churches. Try to schedule some "pulpit exchanges" or periodically swap worship teams. Keep inviting new converts to come share their testimonies.

Send representatives to visit the daughter church especially for special occasions such as baptisms. Plan interaction events with the two congregations – perhaps a combined church concert, picnic, dinner, softball game, or whatever else seems appropriate.

Remember that it's human nature to overestimate your own sacrifice and to underrate the hard work that others do. Both mother and daughter churches can fall for this temptation. The biblical antidote is to heed Paul's wise counsel to "honor one another above yourselves" (Romans 12:10). Everyone should go out of their way to show appreciation for the sacrifices everyone made to plant the new congregation.

Build a relationship with your daughter that will continue to bring you satisfaction over the years. You'll be glad you did.

Pray for Unintentional Daughtering Opportunities (Surprise Pregnancies). In Chapter One we wrote about two basic kinds of daughter church plants: intentional and unintentional. The *STTARR* Process focuses on doing intentional daughtering – planned pregnancies. However, even while you plant a daughter church you may find unexpected opportunities for unintentional daughter church planting. Be ready to receive unintentional pregnancies as gifts from God. Pray for sensitivity to what God is doing, and wisdom in guiding any surprise pregnancies He may provide.

People may approach you to help plant a church in another community or to reach another target group such as *Generation X* or retired people. People might ask for your help to start an "ethnic" or "foreign language" church. Staff members or core team members may get a vision to plant churches of their own. Neighboring churches might ask you to assist them as a partner church in their church planting venture.

Pray and don't be surprised at how God uses you to plant unintentional daughter churches. He may do something you never expected through a wonderful "surprise pregnancy."

Allow Enough Recovery Time Before Your Next Intentional Daughter Plant. Without question, giving birth to a daughter church will take a toll on the mother church. The more you invest the more of a toll it will take. And no matter what size investment you make, your sacrifice will probably require some recovery time before you're ready to give birth again. Even so, overall, we believe that most churches should set a goal to daughter every one to two years, even if they have not fully recovered from the last daughter church plant. God will honor and bless churches that rise to this challenge.

Remember That The Souls Are Worth The Sacrifice, and Start Again With Step One.
After sacrificially giving birth to one daughter church, it might be tempting to think you have done your part and to stop daughtering. We are glad that after planting one church, the Apostle Paul didn't quit. Instead, his attitude was that the souls are worth the sacrifices. Paul wrote, "I make myself a slave to everyone, to win as many as possible" (1 Corinthians 9:19b).

Over time the mother church will return to its normal ministry business and may tend to forget about the daughter and the work being done there. But don't let that happen. Especially celebrate the salvations, since that is why we plant daughter churches.

So plant another daughter church. Just as the job of evangelism never ends, so the job of daughter church planting is a pursuit that won't end until Jesus returns. And what a wonderful pursuit!

With all your experience, the next daughter church will probably be easier. God has stretched your faith, and you have learned a great deal about how to depend upon Him. Most important of all, by becoming a mother church, you have tapped into the most biblical and powerful force for world evangelism!

Let me close by sharing with you an actual note sent to a mother church pastor by a woman who initially opposed the idea of daughtering. She sent this note of thanks after she eventually joined the Core Team.

Dear Pastor Phil,

I am thanking God for you today because on Sunday four people accepted Jesus as their Savior at Spring Valley. I praise God for His sovereignty. Placing the vision of planting churches on your heart has changed people's lives for eternity. You see, if you were not obedient to His call on your life, John, Kay, Carol and Tracy would not have a new life in Christ today. So if you ever stop to question why you are planting churches, please remember that God is expanding His Kingdom because of your obedience. Thank you, Pastor Phil, for your vision, generosity of giving people and resources, and your faithfulness.

Blessings to you and you family,
J. P.

Chapter 10

Your Biological Clock is Ticking

As I write I am sitting in our family's living room listening to classical music and the tic-toc of our mantle clock. Every half hour it chimes and reminds me of the passing of time.

About two hours ago an ambulance pulled up in front of our home and picked up my mother-in-law. She and dad live in our home. It is not the first time we have had to use ambulance services and I am pretty sure it will not be the last. She will likely recover and live for a while longer...who knows how long. Who knows "how long" any of us have? It was eleven years ago this very day (when I was 39) that my mother died suddenly of a "heart attack," the worst day of my life.

All this reminds me that our time on earth is limited. Likewise, for the bride of Christ entrusted to us, the biological clock is ticking. The time to reach the lost is *now*. The time to reproduce is *now*. If we delay, our opportunity will be lost and generations may be lost. We cannot afford to wait.

THE FATHER OF MODERN MISSIONS

William Carey refused to let anything delay or stand in his way. This is despite the fact that Carey was virtually alone in his conviction that it was the right time for born again Christians to spread the Gospel around the world. His fellow pastors in England disagreed. The prevailing outlook in the late 1700's was that the Great Commission pertained only to the original Apostles. They believed that the Apostles had taken the Gospel to the ends of the then-known world and that if later generations were without the Gospel, it was their own fault.

When Carey proposed to a gathering of pastors that the Great Commission was still in force and must be obeyed, Dr. John C. Ryland responded, "Young man, sit down. When God pleases to convert the heathen, He will do it without your aid or mine."[3] Carey dutifully took his seat...but he did not give up his vision for reaching the lost.

Still today there are voices that tell us not to be concerned with lost people around the world and that we can delay in daughtering churches. These voices, from our own thoughts or from others, say things like:

- Spreading the Gospel by daughtering will cost too much money.

- God doesn't need me or my church in order to get the job done.

- There are too many dangers and risks.

- Wait until you have more money, people, facilities, momentum, less conflict, and so on.

WILLIAM CAREY (1761-1834) [4]
"THE FATHER OF MODERN MISSIONS"

So why should we urgently carry the Gospel to the lost around the world? One of the many passages that speak to this issue is Romans 10:9-15.

THE CLEAR PATH OF SALVATION

Romans 10:9-13 gives the clear path of salvation:

> That if you confess with your mouth, "Jesus is Lord," and believe in your heart that God raised him from the dead, you will be saved. For it is with your heart that you believe and are justified, and it is with your mouth that you confess and are saved. As the Scripture says, "Anyone who trusts in him will never be put to shame." For there is no difference between Jew and Gentile-- the same Lord is Lord of all and richly blesses all who call on him, for, "Everyone who calls on the name of the Lord will be saved."

The way to be saved is abundantly clear in these verses. You will be saved if you:

1. Confess with your mouth that "Jesus is Lord." (10:9)
2. Believe in your heart that God raised Jesus from the dead. (10:9)

If by chance you have not yet done this, why not do so right now? Your eternity hangs in the balance.

THE CLEAR PATH OF OUTREACH

That plan of salvation is the most important news in the world. But how can people learn of it? Romans 10:14-15 give the clear **path of outreach:**

> How, then, can they call on the one they have not believed in? And how can they believe in the one of whom they have not heard? And how can they hear without someone preaching to them? And how can they preach unless they are sent? As it is written, "How beautiful are the feet of those who bring good news!"

Again the path is clearly laid out. While, "Everyone who calls on the name of the Lord will be saved" (10:13)…

1. To call, people must first *believe*. (10:14)
2. To believe, people must first *hear*. (10:14)
3. To hear, people must first *be preached to*. (10:14)
4. To preach, people must first *be sent*. (10:15)

The bottom line is that we must *send* people out in order to reach the lost. If they are not sent, then they can't hear preaching, believe and be saved. Where do they have to be sent? By now, hopefully you know that the Great Commission was to Jerusalem (home town), Judea (home region), Samaria (close by but culturally distant) and the uttermost part of the earth. Are you sending people from your church to these four regions?

Those who are sent have "beautiful feet" (10:15). From time to time my wife mentions that I have "ugly feet." (She mostly likes the rest of me.) I strongly disagree, based not only on my own good taste, but on the passage above. She says I have ugly feet, but God says I have beautiful feet, when I share the Good News.

There is no question that William Carey had beautiful feet. Despite ridicule and opposition,

Carey persisted. On May 31, 1792 he delivered a classic sermon based on Isaiah 54:2-3, "Enlarge the place of your tent, stretch your tent curtains wide, do not hold back; lengthen your cords, strengthen your stakes. For you will spread out to the right and to the left; your descendants will dispossess nations and settle in their desolate cities" (NIV). It was in that message that he gave the now famous couplet:

William Carey's Challenge:
"Expect great things from God; attempt great things for God."

Soon after, the poverty-stricken English pastors stepped out in faith to form, "The Particular Baptist Society for Propagating the Gospel Among the Heathen." (They liked long names in those days.) The following year, after overcoming incredible obstacles, Carey sailed for India as the first missionary for this new agency. He served there for forty one years. His labors and letters spawned other missionary efforts both on the European continent and in the USA. He certainly deserves the title, "The Father of Modern Missions." [5]

Since that time, multitudes of missionaries have gone around the world to reach the lost. Their life stories are exciting and challenging.[6] What remarkable commitment and sacrifice. What heroes.

CANNIBALS FOR CHRIST

One of my missionary heroes had the same last name as mine: John Williams. In 1816 he and his wife Mary left England for the Polynesian Islands to spread the Good News to the fierce cannibals who sacrificed their children to the many gods they worshiped. A few islands had been dramatically changed by the Gospel, but there were thousands more waiting for someone to come and teach them about the Savior.

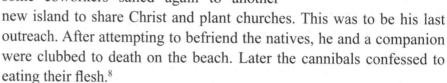

John Williams helped Polynesians get saved, discipled and sent out to plant churches on neighboring islands. Thousands were converted through his undying efforts. Despite hardships, including the death of

seven children who either were stillborn or died soon after birth, his vision of reaching the islanders for Christ never wavered.

Then in 1839 at age 43, Williams and some coworkers sailed again to another

JOHN WILLIAMS (1796-1839)[7]

new island to share Christ and plant churches. This was to be his last outreach. After attempting to befriend the natives, he and a companion were clubbed to death on the beach. Later the cannibals confessed to eating their flesh.[8]

MARKER AT THE GRAVE OF JOHN WILLIAMS IN WESTERN SAMOA[9]

But praise God, the death of John Williams inspired many more Polynesians to take the gospel to neighboring islands and plant churches. Eventually the gospel was spread across the islands of the Western Pacific.

DAUGHTER CHURCH PLANTING IN A WAR ZONE

There are thousands of remarkable missionaries who have suffered similar incredible hardships and sometimes been martyred to advance the Gospel. Likewise there are believers around the world today making great sacrifices to spread the Good News and plant churches.

In March of 2002 two colleagues and I traveled to Ivory Coast in West Africa. There we trained over 200 church planters with our friend Pastor David Boakai, a recent war refugee from nearby Liberia. We visited his humble church of Liberian war refugees. Despite extremely limited resources and virtually no funding, that church planted daughter churches to reach the lost in surrounding villages. Some have "buildings" with plastic for walls and tin roofs. Others have simply a grass roof and a dream of someday owning a building.

DAVID BOAKAI'S CHURCH HAD TARPAPER AND PLASTIC WALLS WITH A TIN ROOF

THIS DAUGHTER CHURCH HAD ONLY A GRASS ROOF (DAVID IN FRONT ROW)

THIS GRANDAUGHTER CHURCH HAD HALF A ROOF!

In the fall of that year rebel insurgents invaded their refugee town of Dananae. David and his family and other Liberians were forced to flee on foot back to their homeland in Liberia. Most possessions were left behind. Soon the fighting also spread to Liberia. David's wife Henrietta's mother died during the war. But through it all David's commitment to planting churches is unwavering.

WHAT GOD COULD DO THROUGH YOU

"GOD is always on the alert, constantly on the lookout for people who are totally committed to him" (2 Chronicles 16:9a). Will you be one of God's champions who are totally committed to him? Will you jump into daughter church planting? God is looking for people committed to spreading the Gospel right now; doing whatever it takes to utilize the most effective method of evangelism and the most biblical method of evangelism—church planting, done in the most effective way—via daughter church planting.

Note: This section is challenging. God has used the following scenarios to motivate many to accomplish more for God. So please read with an open mind and heart, asking the Lord to lead you to His vision, whatever that might be.

If you live in a region where there is great persecution or limited receptivity to the gospel, adjust your outlook accordingly. Your goals might need to be scaled differently, but the Lord can still use you to do more than you might imagine. Let Him stretch your dreams and vision. Read with the following question: How can I dream bigger for God?

A specific question to ponder: "How many people will your church reach for Jesus over the next 15 years?"

Here are four possible responses:

SCENARIO ONE: ADDITION
You might reach 450 people for Christ in fifteen years

In this case, your church might win people to Christ and add them to the church each year. How many converts might that be? Many churches baptize only ten or so converts each year. However, let's suppose that your church wins thirty people to Christ each year for the next fifteen years. That would result in 450 people saved. (15 years x 30 people)

That would be a wonderful accomplishment. It is something that many or most churches won't accomplish over the next fifteen years. Yet we should still strive for it, and more! Here is how we can do more:

SCENARIO TWO: MULTIPLICATION
You might reach 28,350 people for Christ through fifteen years of church multiplication.

Imagine as in the first scenario, your church wins thirty people each year, but also plants churches that plant churches, one every three years and these new churches also reach 450 people in their first fifteen years. There would be sixty-two new churches that would reach a total of 27,900 people for Christ (62 churches x 450 converts = 27,900). Add to that the 450 people your mother church reaches and the total is 28,350!

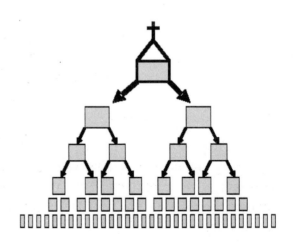

MULTIPLICATION WORKS, IN MATH AND IN CHURCHES

Some might think this is unrealistic, but it is actually quite achievable; the estimates are fairly conservative. Throughout this book are stories of churches that have done much more than this. If you doubt that it could work for you, remember, "God can do anything, you know—far more than you could ever imagine or guess or request in your wildest dreams!" (Eph 3:20).

Consider the Capitol City Baptist Church of Manila in the Philippines which celebrated its silver anniversary in 1984. It had been started in 1959 through a home Bible study group and led many people to the Lord. But it did not just add—it multiplied: daughter, granddaughter and great-granddaughter churches. Over the 25 years it has produced a family tree of 37 congregations. It would have been easy for the church leaders to excuse themselves: "This is a developing country, we need to grow the mother church instead of planting daughter churches, and God has called missionaries to evangelize here – not us." But they overcame the mental obstacles and reaped a great harvest for Christ.

God is looking for leaders like Isaiah who recorded, "Then I heard the voice of the Lord saying, 'Whom shall I send? And who will go for us?' And I said, 'Here am I. Send me!'" (Isaiah 6:8) Will you step out and multiply?

SCENARIO THREE: INFLUENCE-MULTIPLICATION
You might reach 56,700 people for Christ in fifteen years

If you become a multiplier of multipliers, you can dramatically increase your Kingdom impact. What does that mean? An Influence Multiplier influences another church to begin multiplying churches. If you influence one other church to do as you do, you can potentially **double** your impact in church multiplication. Instead of reaching some 28,350 people using the projections above, you could influence another church to do the same thing and therefore double the impact to 56,700.

How do I know this is possible? Because my church planting mentor Dr. Bob Logan influenced me to begin daughtering. Bob looked me in the eye and said something like, "Mark, it's great that your church plant is doing well, but now you also need to start planting churches." Then he explained why.

To my shame, I admit that I cringed when Bob challenged me. I was quite uncomfortable because I had worked so hard to build my own church and the thought of "giving away" some of my resources, especially "my" people, was very difficult to imagine. I had sweated and slaved to start and build my church. To send some out to start another church was a bad thought. I wanted to build "my" own church.

But the more I prayed about it more, the more I realized Bob was right. I had to admit it that:

- Church planting is the **most Biblical** method of evangelism
- Church planting is the **most effective** method of evangelism
- And the **most effective way** to plant churches is daughter church planting

The Holy Spirit's conviction was clear. How could I not do it? I had to shift my focus to the bigger picture. From addition to multiplication. From "My kingdom come, my will be done" to "Thy kingdom come, thy will be done."

I am very glad Bob challenged me! If you can do for someone what Bob did for me, you might double your impact.

How could you influence other churches? You might:

- ❖ Share the vision with your association or denomination
- ❖ Share this book with friends
- ❖ Speak to your pastor's fellowship
- ❖ Challenge leaders individually
- ❖ Help initiate a goal for church planting in your association

SCENARIO FOUR: FIFTH DEGREE INFLUENCE-MULTIPLICATION
You might reach 141,750 people for Christ in fifteen years

If instead of just one, you influence five others to plant churches that multiply, the total saved through those five multiplying networks could be 141,750 (28,350 x 5). What an impact. Yet it is achievable through multiplication. In fact, there are many leaders around the world who are having this kind of impact and far more, as they have joined hands with others in the vision of church multiplication.

Years ago a series of black and white photos in *Life* magazine portrayed a gripping story. The first photo was of a dimly lit kitchen with a weeping mother surrounded by comforting friends. The previous day when she turned her back for a few moments, her 3 year old son wandered into the wheat fields of her Nebraska wheat farm. Too small to be seen among the wheat stalks, the parents searched all day. At dusk they called their neighbors and throughout the night searched with flashlights and lanterns.

Finally at dawn more than 50 people joined hands to make a human chain and sweep through the fields. At about noon they found the boy who had died from exposure to the elements.

The last photo showed the father, his face streaked with dirt and sweat, carrying his lifeless son home. He was quoted, "If only we had joined hands sooner, he could have been saved."

Will you join hands with others so the Lost might be saved?

SCENARIO FIVE: OVER THE TOP INFLUENCE-MULTIPLICATION
Who knows how many people you might reach?

Because I have the privilege of rubbing shoulders with top level church planting leaders, I have gotten to know some of the greatest STTARRS of our day.

Pastor Phil Spry from Raleigh-Durham, North Carolina was saved in his early 20s. Phil has personally planted six churches. He started his current church plant in 1997. After about 18 months they began sending out daughter church planters. There are several now and their combined attendance exceeds that of the mother church.

Phil has also started a ministry called Tellstart (www.tellstart.com) which utilizes computers to make phone calls for new church starts. Tellstart has helped plant over 400 churches, with Phil usually mentoring their pastors through the process of planting via phone. He also teaches church planting in seminars and has written resources for church planters. He has impacted hundreds of new churches. Through influence multiplication, Phil has helped to reach thousands and thousands of people for Christ.

Dr. Jayakumar Ramachandran of Bangalore, India, is another world-class Influence Multiplier. He is the founding pastor of Calvary's Grace Bible Church, which is a mother church currently involved in 11 daughter church plants in the state of Karnataka. Many of these churches have been started by graduates of the Bible college and seminary he founded, The Academy for Church Planting and Leadership. They have been sent out through his organization; Bible Believing Churches and Missions. Currently 43 staff members serve in and around India with him. That is remarkable influence multiplication in another developing nation.

Paul Becker is the founder and president of the mission I serve, Dynamic Church Planting International. Paul planted four churches in his early ministry and then began writing and mentoring other church planters. He started our mission in 1995 and in ten years it has trained thousands of church planters, produced written resources for church planters and we estimate it has impacted the planting of over 13,000 church plants. Most of the multiplication is through our Certified Trainers (CT's) who are trained to train others using our materials. Once qualified, they are given all of our training resources and sent out to multiply the training around the world. Our vision is to eventually equip some 5,000 of these leaders to impact the planting of a million churches.

You may have never heard of these leaders before. However, in heaven God's greatest rewards will be for those who have maximized their talents to reach the lost for Christ and who "lead many to righteousness." They will not necessarily be the ones who have the biggest "names" in the Christian world.

In fact, Jesus warned about popularity saying in Luke 6:26, "Woe to you when all men speak well of you, for that is how their fathers treated the false prophets." Eugene Peterson paraphrased this verse in *The Message*, "There's trouble ahead when you live only for the approval of others, saying what flatters them, doing what indulges them. Popularity contests are not truth contests-- look how many scoundrel preachers were approved by your ancestors! Your task is to be true, not popular." Influence Multipliers don't follow the path of popularity; they follow the path of truth. Jesus commendation "well done thou good and faithful servant" will be for leaders like these.

YOUR COMMITMENT

I hope you are or will become an Influence Multiplier. My dream is that you, with whatever resources and abilities you have, will maximize your impact for Christ by multiplying your church and influencing others to do the same. Imagine what can happen if enough of us decide to do so.

In the song "Imagine" John Lennon got the formula wrong, but at least he had a vision:

> You may say I'm a dreamer
> But I'm not the only one
> I hope someday you'll join us
> And the world will live as one

After reading this book, you have the correct formula for changing the world. Now I hope you will join us—those working to win the world for Christ through the most effective and most biblical strategy: daughter church planting.

Will you take the challenge? Here is your opportunity to commit to four levels of involvement, please check the ones that apply to your commitment level at this time:

I WILL PRAY

I commit to pray for church planting *and* about whether or not God wants me to have a part in daughter church planting.

I WILL HELP

If presented with an opportunity, I commit to assist in a new church plant in whatever way(s) I can, such as: being a core team member, giving financially, encouraging people from my church to help out, going door-to-door, etc.

I WILL PLANT

I commit to proactively work to multiply churches: by leading my church to daughter, by starting a church planting committee in my church, by seeking out an opportunity to join the Launch Team of a new church, by becoming a church planting staff team member, etc.

I WILL MULTIPLY

I commit to proactively work to influence other churches to begin to multiply churches (influence-multiplication): by inviting others to participate, by sharing the vision, by sharing this book with others, by speaking on the topic to groups of concerned Christians, and so on.

LAYING IT ALL DOWN

C.T. Studd (1860-1931) was the son of a wealthy businessman in England. While in China as a missionary at age 25 he received word of a huge inheritance. Instead of indulging himself, or securing his future, Studd gave the entire sum to ministry, except a smaller amount which he presented to his bride just before their marriage. She in turn gave that entire amount to ministry as well. They gave the rest of their lives to missionary service in China, India and Africa.[10]

C.T. Studd's Challenge:
"The gamblers for gold are many, but the gamblers for God are few.
Where are the gamblers for God?"

God may not be calling you or me to a foreign mission field or to give away our entire fortune. But what is he asking us to do? Is it not possible that he is asking us to break out of our fellowship walls and multiply churches to reach the lost?

C.T. Studd's Philosophy:
"Some want to live within the sound of church or chapel bell;
I want to run a rescue shop within a yard of hell."

CHAPTER SUMMARY

In this chapter, we have looked at the mandate to spread the Gospel. We've been reminded that while there are many excuses and many who excuse themselves from missions responsibility, the Lord will reward those who fulfill His Great Commission and plant churches. We have seen the power of multiplication and hopefully you have made decisions about being a multiplier.

Prayer Points: How you can pray about the concepts in this chapter:

- Pray that leaders will listen and not be closed-minded.
- Pray that God will strengthen you as you seek to fulfill your commitments above.
- Pray that the Gospel will advance throughout the world through church planting.
- Pray for missionaries who are putting everything on the line to spread the gospel
- Pray for more influence multipliers to advance the Gospel without regard to personal gain.
- Pray about who you can influence.

Action Steps: What you can do to begin to implement the steps in this chapter.

- Study the points in this chapter.
- Prayerfully make and fulfill your commitments at the end of this chapter.
- Acquire a copy of *The Dynamic Daughter Church Planting Handbook* and study so you can be as successful as possible in planting daughter churches. (Available at www.dcpi.org)
- Give copies of this book to friends who might work with you to accomplish your vision.

---

[1] Joe S. McIlhaney, Jr., M.D. with Susan Nethery, *1250 Health-Care Questions Women Ask*, (Baker Book House, Grand Rapids, 1985), p. 365.

[2] Article in the *Baptist Courier*, February 8, 1996, p. 4.

[3] J. Herbert Kane, *Understanding Christian Missions* (Grand Rapids: Baker Book House, revised edition, 1978), p. 147.

[4] www.wholesomewords.org/ echoes/carey.html

[5] Kane, p. 148.

[6] An entire series of missionary biographies titled "Christian Heroes Then and Now" by Janet and Geoff Benge, published by YWAM Publishing, are easy to read, yet challenging for both youth and adults. www.ywampublishing.com. 1-800-922-2143.

[7] www.urc.org.uk/archive_ frontpage/pilots/

[8] Janet and Geoff Benge, *John Williams: Messenger of Peace* (Seattle: YWAM Publishing, 2002), p. 194.

[9] www.galenfrysinger.com/ apia.htm

[10] http://www.wholesomewords.org/missions/biostudd.html

Other Books by Dr. Mark Alan Williams

The New Dynamic Church Planting Handbook
by Paul Becker, Jim Carpenter and Mark Williams

The Dynamic Daughter Church Planting Handbook
by Paul Becker and Mark Williams

How to Develop a Leadership Board for Your New Church
by Paul Becker and Mark Williams

Finding Start-up Facilities for Your New Church
by Mark Williams

All of these resources are available from
Dynamic Church Planting Resources
Oceanside, California, USA
www.dcpi.org
service@dcpi.org
Phone: 800-255-0431